EVERYDAY MAGIC

Gina Mazzone

EVERYDAY MAGIC

ISBN: 978-1-7363811-0-6

Dedication

In honor of my mother Marilyn Jean.

You are, and always have been, the wind beneath my wings.

EVERYDAY MAGIC

CONTENTS

EVERYDAY MAGIC

Introduction

There is a stream of Divine Love and Infinite Intelligence flowing through all creation. When you align your energy with this greater part of you, you have the ability to transform your life in any way you choose.

I have desired, for some time now, to write a book on ways to realize personal transformation in various areas of life. I have personally experienced the awe in watching things manifest into my experience when applying the principles and techniques that I have summarized for you in this book. My intention for this book is to assist you in taking creative control in your life and give you the fundamental knowledge and skills necessary to manifest your heart's desires.

I have been a student of these teachings for over forty years, and I have read numerous books and taken many workshops in all areas of personal development. My personal growth has always been a priority, and I never tire of the constant reinforcement of ways to improve myself as well as my experiences. This book is a culmination of everything I have learned from many great teachers, along with my personal experience in applying this knowledge to my life.

I was first introduced to these teachings in 1977. I was fourteen years old when my mom gave me the book *How to use the Science of Mind*, by Earnest Holmes. When I first read the book it immediately resonated with me. I'm not sure if it was because I was so young and open minded, or if it was something that I felt I already knew on some deeper level. Either way, it was the first step on a life-transforming journey that I am still on today. The basic premise of that book was that thought is creative, and through correct use of your thoughts you can affect your experiences and have the power to transform your life. I immediately gravitated to this concept. I loved the idea that I had creative power through my thinking, which in turn, gave me creative control in my life.

The first big demonstration of my ability to use transformative thinking was when I envisioned my first car. I can still recall riding my bicycle and visualizing that I was driving my own car, stating positive affirmations, and really believing anything was possible. Sure enough, by the time I turned sixteen, I bought a 1970 Ford Mustang from my older brother for $800. Keep in mind, I was raised by a single mom, so I earned every penny of that $800 myself. I was also responsible for the cost of insurance and all other expenses related to owning and maintaining the vehicle. Now obviously, the car didn't just materialize out of thin air. I did get a job and worked for it, but it was these teachings that motivated me and inspired me to believe in myself. I started working at the age of fourteen and I lied to my employers about my age to get my first job. It was at a hot dog stand for $2.00 per hour and minimum wage was $2.65 at that time. Within several months I was hired at a new job selling shoes for $3.00 an hour plus commission, so I became a believer in the power of positive thinking at an incredibly young age.

I am truly diverse when it comes to religion and spirituality. I was raised in the Christian Catholic faith and then was introduced to Religious Science (not to be mistaken with Scientology) in my teens. At one point, I was engaged to marry a Jewish man and was planning on raising my children in the Jewish faith. I also enjoy learning about Eastern philosophies such as Taoism, Buddhism, and Hinduism, and currently I have gravitated to Joel Osteen. I just love his spirit, passion, and positive message. I try to keep an open mind, and I am drawn to teachings that resonate in my heart.

I'm not here to challenge your religious or spiritual beliefs, and if anything I am suggesting makes you feel uncomfortable, then follow your own inner guidance. It is not my intention to persuade anyone into accepting my views, I am just sharing my own unique perspective and bless all in having the courage to explore and live your own truth as well. There are many paths to spirituality. It's important that you find a path that resonates with who you are, and brings you the joy, love, prosperity, and creative self-expression, you came here to experience.

CHAPTER 1
The Magic Potion

The Universe is not outside of you. Look inside yourself.
Everything you want you already are. Rumi

What is this "Magic Potion?" It's a fun easy to use formula that I designed to assist you in transforming your energy and your life. It contains all the components of the Creative Process which can be used to create the life you have always dreamed of. The Magic Potion consists of six ingredients, and you can begin by using whichever one you want. You will begin seeing immediate results as you apply these ingredients.

You will just need to start with an open mind, and a willingness to evaluate your life, including how you perceive it and participate in it. It will also require discipline and patience as it is a never-ending process. At times, you may feel challenged, but if you stick with it, you will start to see your life transforming and you will begin enjoying being a powerful creator in your world.

In this chapter, I will briefly review all the ingredients. Then in the following chapters, I will expand on each one providing you with a more in-depth understanding, as well as some tools and exercises to assist you in applying these principles in your everyday life. It is the application of these principles that will bring you the changes and desires you want to manifest. An Ancient Chinese proverb teaches, "Talk does not cook rice." Real transformation comes from "living" your life, not just analyzing it. It's through your participation and exploration in life that you will grow and evolve, and experience all the beauty, mystery and magic that is available to you.

Knowledge and awareness are great starting points, but some people never move beyond this. It is my intention with this book to assist you in moving beyond self-awareness to personal empowerment, encouraging you to release the past and put your energy into creating your future and the life you envision for yourself. Progression is the goal, not perfection. You are going to make mistakes, and that's ok. Sometimes it may be scary leaving your comfort zone or challenging some of your beliefs, but you can't expect to have different results in your life if you keep doing things the same way. Experiment with it, have fun with it, and know that it's a never-ending journey. Remember that the primary goal is to enjoy the ride.

The basic underlying principle of this book is that all

change starts from within. To have any real and lasting changes in your experiences, or in your behavior, you must first start with your inner world. Imagine a projector casting an image on a wall in your home, it may be an unfulfilling relationship, limited finances, a self-sabotaging behavior, or any other negative condition. If you wanted to change the image, would you proceed to tear down the wall? No, because you realize that the projector is still going to project the same image regardless if the wall is there or not. Yet, when we want to make changes in our lives, so many of us start by tearing down the wall, attempting to change the people and experiences in our world, without ever looking at the projector and the movie that is playing.

The ingredients of the Magic Potion primarily consist of what is necessary to create a new movie, therefore projecting a new image on the wall. Each ingredient stands on its own, meaning it is not necessary to combine all the ingredients before you start to see changes in your experience. Even by just applying one of the components you can start on your journey. The more you work with each one, the more you will see your life changing, and more importantly you will experience more joy, love, and fulfillment in your life. Here is an introduction to each ingredient, which will be followed by an entire chapter devoted to each one.

The Ingredients

Desire: The first ingredient is desire. It is the point where creation begins and inherent in the desire is all the intelligence necessary for its manifestation. Desire is the seed of creation and without desire there is no physical world. Desire motivates action and thought which in turn affect your vibration, which is your point of attraction.

The Universal Field: Once the desire is born it is released into the Universal Field of Infinite Possibilities, and what becomes of that desire will depend on how you nurture it. Think of it like planting a seed. This Universal Field is like the soil, and your thoughts, actions and emotions will determine how that desire unfolds. The Law of Attraction is in this field and is bringing to you a match to your thoughts, beliefs, and emotions.

Thoughts: Thinking allows us to make sense of and interpret the world in which we live. All thoughts are not creative, but they do have the potential to be, so it is especially important to make sure you are monitoring them. What you are thinking affects your emotional vibration which determines your attraction point, so it is best to be thinking positive, uplifting thoughts. It is also how you mold the details of your desire and create the image of what you would like to experience.

Emotions: Your emotions are an indicator of your point of attraction and are what the Law of Attraction is responding to. We think thousands of thoughts per day, but the thoughts backed by emotions are going to have the strongest creative power whether they be positive or negative.

Beliefs: A belief can be described as a state of mind in which a person thinks something to be true, without there being evidence to support it. We all have a variety of beliefs on different subjects. Our beliefs are usually inherited from our family, society, or life experiences and we just accept them without question. They are a driving force determining how we experience life and a very powerful component in our point of attraction.

Action: Action is the final ingredient, and I would say probably the least important of all the other ingredients. This does not mean you should not go out there and participate in life. What it does mean is that when you focus solely on taking action without looking at your attraction point, you may end up spinning your wheels. Aligning your energy and vibration is always the first step in manifesting your desires. No amount of action on its own can supersede your energetic attraction point.

So now you have the ingredients for the "Magic Potion." For many years I have been studying these ideas and principles and wanted to put it all together in a simple to use formula. And although the understanding of it can be simple, applying it to your life is not always easy. I can promise you though, that if you take the information being offered in this book, and apply these principles, you will see your life transform. At first it may feel a little like "Magic" but after time you will start to build confidence in yourself and in the Creative Process. Then it will start to feel as natural as breathing, or what I like to call Everyday Magic.

CHAPTER 2
Desire

You are what your deep driving desire is. As your desire is, so is your will. As your will is, so is your deed. As your deed is, so is your destiny. **Brihadaranyaka Upanishad IV.4.5**

Desire is the first ingredient in the Magic Potion and the driving force behind all creation. It is not something that you need to search for in the outside world but emerges from within. It is a natural response to interacting with your world, and when aligned with your inner being, it can propel you forward creating a life of fulfillment and joy. Some philosophies and religions warn against desires and suggest eliminating them or trying to tame our desire to live happier lives, but nothing could be farther from the truth. It can be true that in the pursuit of our desires, we can sometimes lose site of the vision we have for our lives and get lost in illusions. Therefore, it is important to understand our desires, appreciate them and discover the gift contained within them.

It is impossible to live a life without desire as desires are continuously being born throughout your day, all day long. You get up in the morning and look in the mirror and want to be thinner. While getting ready you hear an ad on the radio for a dream vacation you have always wanted to take. On your way to work you pass by a restaurant you have been wanting to check out for some time. When you get to work your boss gives you a hard time and you wish he would appreciate you more. Later that evening you meet a friend who is habitually late, and you would like them to be more respectful of your time. As you can see there's no way to prevent desires from being born, nor should you want to. It has been said that desire can be the cause of suffering, and there may be some truth in that, but trying to eliminate your desires is not the answer.

It is not the desire that causes the suffering, but your relationship with the desire that can cause the distress. The main thing that creates the discord within you is that you feel your desire is unattainable or will be difficult to experience. This is usually where a lot of the inner conflict lies. We feel that our desires will not be fulfilled, or when we get what we want, we might lose it, or someone may take it away. It is not the desire, but our feeling of lack and powerlessness that creates the inner conflict. So, the first step is to become in harmony with your desire, and you will be learning how to do that throughout this book. For now, it's important for you to understand that first it is impossible to not have desires, and second, it is when we are not in harmony with our desire that we feel unfulfilled and dissatisfied.

Harmonize With Your Desires

Desires are a normal, healthy response to life, but they can be misleading if not properly understood. Let's take a look at one of the examples I gave earlier. The first example was looking in the mirror and wanting to be thinner. The question you want to ask yourself is why do you want to be thinner? Is it because you want to feel better about yourself, or you think your partner may love you more? Or, if you do not have a partner do you feel that being thinner will bring you one? Is it to feel healthier or to fit in the clothes you have hanging in your closet? In looking at these reasons we can see that what you truly desire is to love yourself, feel loved and to express more life and joy in your experience. You are thinking that being thinner is going to create those feelings, but in reality there is no guarantee that it will. To be in harmony with your desire you first want to create these emotions and feelings. When you do that your point of attraction shifts and that is what the Law of Attraction is responding to. Now you are becoming a magnet for a multitude of experiences that will generate more of those same feelings.

It is very common when you want to bring something or someone into your experience that you feel empty and disconnected, thinking you cannot feel fulfilled or happy until you attain it. And when you feel that way, that is what the Law of Attraction is responding to, and you will continue to experience feelings of lack and a constant yearning. That is why some people feel that desires can lead to suffering or a constant state of dissatisfaction, but you have the power to change that at any time. Your thoughts, emotions, beliefs, and actions create your energetic atmosphere, and when they are in accord with your desires you feel happy and joyful. This will give the Law of Attraction a powerful signal to respond to and this is how we learn to manifest the life we are dreaming of.

A fun place to start is creating the essence of your desire. When doing this there are a couple of things to keep in mind. First, you always want to be expressing as if the desire has already manifested. This may seem counter intuitive, but the Universe is responding to your energetic setpoint, and you are always creating now in this moment. All your power is always in the present moment. The second thing you want to do is describe how your life would look and feel if you were actually living that experience. Get as detailed as you can, describing the form and why and how this will benefit your life and how it makes you feel.

One of my favorite manifestations was when I bought my first home. I was currently living in a townhome that I owned, but really wanted a single-family home and had a strong vision of what I wanted. I am an architectural designer, so I knew if I found something with the right "bones" I had the ability to transform it. It took me almost two years, but I did end up with my dream home that is absolutely perfect for me in every way.

The first thing I did was come up with a detailed list of everything I wanted in order to give the Universe a blueprint to work from. On the list were my must haves, but I also included some things that would be great but not a necessity. This is what my list looked like:

- Architecturally pleasing exterior, structurally sound and mechanicals in good working condition
- Nice low maintenance private back yard
- Friendly, quiet, and considerate neighbors
- Nature setting, beautiful trees, not too messy and perfectly located
- Convenient to work, highways, social activities and close to my mother
- Fresh vegetable market close by
- Spacious kitchen open to family room
- Fireplace
- Place for exercise equipment
- Home office to work out of with lots of natural light and beautiful views
- Plenty of closet space easy to organize
- Guest bedroom
- Affordable taxes
- Nice size eating area
- At a price I can easily afford

Would be nice to have:

- Convenient laundry area on the first floor
- Mudroom
- Two car garage
- Place for baby grand piano

- Screened porch
- Finished basement

The next thing I did was write out a description of how it would feel to be living in the home as if I were already there:

- I can see myself driving down a beautiful block lined with mature trees and pretty homes, pulling up in my driveway with a feeling of love and appreciation for my beautiful home.
- It's so peaceful and tranquil to sit in my backyard hearing the birds chirp and the wind blowing through the leaves on the trees.
- It's so relaxing sitting by the fireplace and snuggling on my couch.
- Feeling financially free and enjoying an abundant and prosperous life. Having plenty of money to spare and share.
- I love working in my home office overlooking my yard and watching Cherokee (the dog I did not have yet) play in the yard.
- Coming home into a mudroom area that is perfect for the dog to dry off and for me to keep coats and shoes organized.
- I love to cook in my kitchen and there's plenty of storage and counter space. Lots of natural light.
- Waking up in my beautiful master bedroom that fits my bedroom set perfectly. Waking up every day knowing I am in my perfect place.
- My guests really enjoy staying over and are very comfortable and have privacy.

- My bathroom is everything I always wanted and such a joy to get ready in. It's a functional beautiful space with plenty of storage.
- I have the perfect eating area and it's so much fun to have guests over and entertain.
- I get along great with my neighbors, they are so friendly, quiet, and considerate.
- I really like that it's located so close to my mom and work and it's also a great area for biking and walking my dog.
- I absolutely love my home. It's everything I always wanted, and I feel such love and appreciation for this blessing in my life.

These are some fun exercises to get your creative energy flowing. Like anything else in life, the more you do them the better you will be at creating the essence of the desire. As you can see, I focused a lot of my energy on how I would "feel in the experience." This is truly where your greatest power lies. This is what the Law of Attraction is responding to and it's also your personal barometer to see how in harmony you are with your desire. I also was very specific about the form I wanted my desire to take. I then released this to the Infinite Intelligence knowing as long as I can master the essence of the desire, the Universe would match that. Sometimes the form may not be exactly what we envisioned. What we truly want is to feel a certain way in the experience, and by leaving it open to the Creative Intelligence there may be many ways to achieve this.

For instance, on my list of would be nice was a two-car garage and a screened porch. Even though I was living alone and only needed a one car garage, I thought it would be nice to have a bigger garage should I decide to live with someone. And of course, I did not need a screened porch, but loved the idea of being able to sit out at night and avoid the bugs. Although, I did have a hard time visualizing how the porch would flow with the house. I did not want anything off the back obstructing my view of the yard and thought it might look funny off the front of the house. But I put it on the list anyway knowing the Universe is All Knowing and Infinitely Intelligent and turned it over. I was just amazed when I found a home with a detached two- car garage, and half of it was a screened in porch. So, I got my porch in a way that I never imagined, and if someday I should ever need a two-car garage that was a possibility as well. This is a perfect example of releasing a desire to the Universe and being open to the variety of ways it can be fulfilled.

Desire is the seed of creation and within it is all the possibilities for its unfoldment. When you release it to the Field of Infinite Possibilities, it's like planting a seed in the soil and then waiting for it to grow and blossom. Letting go of your limiting beliefs and negative thoughts is like pulling the weeds. Showering it with positive emotions is like watering it and making sure it gets plenty of sunlight. Over time as you apply these principles you will see how very dependable and reliable they are, but you must take the first steps. Once you have some demonstrations it will reinforce your beliefs and that will increase your power of attraction.

The house I attracted was perfect for me in every way. Every day I am so thankful that I have been blessed and I constantly send out thoughts and feelings of love and appreciation for my home. When I purchased the home, it was a major fixer upper, but it had the potential to be everything I dreamed of. Over the years I have transformed it, and it has been amazing to see how it all unfolded and is still unfolding. It has been a wonderful adventure and a great opportunity to continually put these principles into practice.

Misguided Desires

Although our desires come from our inner being that is always wanting to evolve and feel fulfilled, we can sometimes lose our way and get off track. We find ourselves trapped in destructive habits or addictions or "looking for love in all the wrong places," as the saying goes. The most important thing to keep in mind is that even though the desire may be playing out in self-sabotaging and destructive behaviors, the underlying yearning is always wanting to be more and to express our true essence and highest potential. When a person becomes enraged and strikes out at someone or is manipulative and untruthful, it would appear their desire is to hurt someone. But when we look at the underlying motivation behind this behavior, we can see they are in a place of disconnection. They are not acting from the pureness of the desire but from the feeling of lack in having it fulfilled.

When people do harmful things to others it always comes from a place of fear and lack and never from the pureness of the desire and connection with their Higher Power. For example, let's say someone has found out their partner has been unfaithful, and they react in a violent manner. It may seem like their desire was to harm their partner for breaking the agreement they had, but if you look deeper this is really about the fear of losing their partner or the hurt or embarrassment of being deceived. The true desire is to feel they can trust their partner and feel valued and loved. Or if someone is stealing it comes from a place of lack and insecurity, not from the place of feeling they deserve good in their life and feeling loved and provided for by the Unlimited Source of the Universe. Somehow people get off course and engage in behaviors and activities that only amplify the fear and lack and create more of the same.

Addictions are an example of misguided desires as well. When people engage in destructive or compulsive behaviors there is always an underlying cause or what I refer to as a misguided desire. Once you heal that, the addiction will no longer exist. Just withholding from the negative behavior is not enough. So many overweight individuals who get a lap band procedure and reach a more desirable weight, will then find themselves dealing with alcohol, sex, or other addictions that they were not experiencing before. The reason for this is that they did not heal the underlying cause of the addiction and therefore it is just expressing itself in another area.

The main drive behind an addiction is wanting a feeling

of relief from distress and attaining a feeling of connection with the Divine Energy that flows through all creation. People will try to achieve that through altered states which can take the form of substance or process addictions. A substance addiction is the inappropriate use of drugs, over the counter medi-cations, nicotine, alcohol, or even certain foods can be addicting. Process addictions can come in many forms such as shopping, gambling, sex, food, social media, or other internet usage. With substance addictions there is a physical withdrawal that is the first step in freeing yourself from the behavior, and the intensity of this can vary. Behind both substance and process addiction is the mental and emotional addiction, which is usually far more difficult to overcome than the physical withdrawal. It is very common for people who have been free from their addictions for years to revert right back to their old behaviors. That is why it is so important to heal the underlying cause of the addiction. Once you do this, you will no longer have the desire to engage in the destructive behavior or abuse it.

Many members in my family suffered from alcoholism, and I too dealt with substance abuse at a very young age. I remember at the age of fifteen having physical cravings for alcohol around 5:00pm, that was usually when my friends and I started drinking. This quickly progressed to drug abuse as well, so I do have personal experience dealing with addictions. I also was a smoker for over 20 years and can personally attest that the physical withdraw was nothing compared to the mental and emotional addiction that is tied to the behavior. The first time I quit smoking was for three years and I was well beyond the physical addiction when I started up again. It then took me several years until I was able to quit again.

Addictions can destroy lives. If you are suffering from an addiction and want to regain control back in your life it will take commitment and a strong desire to be free from the behavior. Several of my relatives found Alcoholics Anonymous to be a path to healing and I personally witnessed the transformation in their lives from working the program. The program however was not the path for me. I tried going to a couple meetings, read the books, learned about the steps, but I had a hard time saying I was powerless, which is the first step. I am not condemning AA in any way. It saved the lives of people who were very dear to me and has helped so many people lead clean and sober lives.

I think because I had been introduced to the Science of Mind teachings at such a young age, I had a very different take on things. I believed I could have control over drugs and alcohol, and that I could be healed of the addiction. This is very different from AA which teaches you will always be an alcoholic. I believed the destructive behavior was just a symptom of an inner cause, and once that was healed, I would be free from the addiction and still be able to socially drink without having it control me. Now, I was not healed overnight, it took several years of self-reflection and being open to healing and changing my behavior. One thing that really helped me was finding more productive things to do with my time that helped build my self-esteem and strengthen my identity.

First, I put myself through college. My grades were terrible in high school as I was majoring in partying and had no interest in what they were attempting to teach me. When I was able to decide what I wanted to learn, I became committed, applied for student loans, and did graduate with a very high-grade point average. I also became a fitness fanatic, which was a bit of an addiction as well, but at least a healthier one. It's very helpful when you are trying to break a negative habit that you find something to replace the void with. I had structured my time with more positive activities that were helping me develop a new self-image, and they were also things that I truly enjoyed.

At the same time, I also was doing a lot of healing work using affirmations and creative visualization, as well as challenging my belief systems. I was always looking for positive and productive ways to meet life's challenges, as opposed to just trying to escape or avoid them. Over time, this healed my addictive behaviors. Today, I can drink without losing control of my life and I have no desire to do any drugs whatsoever. I'm not saying I never get drunk, but it's very rare, and the reason I drink has changed. In the past I drank to cope with life's stresses and to escape. Now I love being present for my life, and when challenges arise, I do not use alcohol or drugs to numb myself. When we are present in our lives and deal with hardships and heartbreaks we grow and will eventually heal and be stronger and wiser. My favorite poet and philosopher is Kahlil Gibran and in his book *The Profit* he wrote, "Pain is the breaking of the shell that encloses your understanding". Emotional pain, although extremely uncomfortable at times, has the ability to transform us if we open ourselves to the lessons and wisdom it contains.

Evaluating Desires

So how do you know if your desires are misguided? We want to make sure our desires are going to bring us true fulfillment and not just fill a void. How many people do you know who are owned by their possessions? They do not have time to enjoy them because they are too busy working to pay for them. Or they may settle for an unfulfilling relationship because they would rather be with anybody than be alone. Evaluating your desires can be very beneficial and may give you insight as to whether it is something you want to invest your time and energy on. Asking yourself the following questions may be helpful in determining if the desire is something you choose to pursue or not.

Does it feel like inspiration? Am I being pulled toward something, or am I running away or resisting something?

A lot of our desires are born from undesirable cir-cumstances. A dysfunctional relationship, unfulfilling job, health challenges, financial stresses and the list goes on. Desire is a natural response to life when we are dissatisfied and want things to be different or are being inspired to something greater. It can be very helpful to evaluate the energy around the desire. The example I gave earlier about overcoming my addiction is a good illustration. When I started exercising more on a regular basis, I experienced how great it felt to be physically fit and more health conscious. So, when my friends wanted to stay out all night partying it became easier for me to not join them. I was more inspired to get up early and hit the gym. I was no longer fighting or resisting the addiction, I was being drawn to a new behavior that felt great and increased my wellbeing. What we resist persists. Cleaning up the energy around our desires is essential in leading us in the right direction.

Another personal example was my desire to write a book. Although I was not unhappy in my current career choice, I was feeling an inner nudge that was calling me and would not stop no matter how much I would try and ignore it. I questioned my ability and experience to do such a thing for years and then finally gave in. I decided I was going to write this book even if I am the only person that ever reads it. This is not to say that there won't be times in your life that you will want to leave a job or unhealthy relationship or situation, but it's important to really evaluate your motives. Once you get a clear understanding of what you want and why you want it, you can put your energy and time on creating the new experience as opposed to pushing against the unwanted one. You will eventually get to the point where you are grateful for the negative experience because it is motivating you to make the changes in your life, which creates a sense of personal empowerment and wellbeing.

Am I people-pleasing or enabling others?

A great question to ask yourself is "Is this something I want or is it someone else's expectation of me?" When we love people it's natural to find joy in pleasing them and giving of our self, so it's important to decipher what is motivating the desire. If we are desiring something because we feel others will approve of us, we want them to love us more, or we in some way feel guilt or responsible for them, we really want to take a closer look. A lot of times underneath our desire is a need to control the person, or a need to be needed. Giving of yourselves to others is a wonderful thing, you just want to make sure it's coming from a place of joy and love.

Enabling others is unhealthy for both parties even though your intentions may be good. When we do for others what they should be doing for themselves we cripple them and make them dependent on us. Even though we may be truly wanting to help the person we have to realize that they are responsible for their own happiness and wellbeing. We may know how to solve their problems, but this is something they need to learn on their own. Life is like a classroom and when we try to do others' homework, we are not truly helping them. When we enable others, we are usually creating resentments and conflict in the relationship. There is an old saying that "The rescuer becomes the next victim." We need to make sure when we are desiring good things for others that we are not interfering with their growth and independence.

We may think that the person will love us more but deep down they may feel dependent and weak and then blame us. They might also feel manipulated and controlled so it's very important that we carefully examine our feelings behind these desires to "help" others. When our desire for others is pure and not clouded by control, guilt, or manipulation it feels free. We are not doing it because we are expecting something in return, we are doing it simply to experience the joy and love that it brings to us. We are not cleaning up their mess, but seeing them as capable, self-sufficient individuals and trusting their ability to take care of themselves.

Am I making others responsible for my happiness?

When we make others responsible for our happiness or wellbeing, we give our power away. This can be tricky in relationships and friendships as we tend to have certain expectations as to how we want to be treated as we become involved with these individuals. I am in no way suggesting that you stay in an unfulfilling or unhealthy relationship. So many people will go from one relationship to another, just to find the same struggles they were experiencing in the previous relationship. If we don't clear our energy up we may end up attracting similar situations again and again. As long as you wait for others to create your happiness or fill some internal void, you are setting yourself up for a letdown.

It's unfortunate, but our society tends to set us up for this disappointment. Remember the unforgettable line in the movie Jerry McGuire, "You complete me" As heartwarming, dramatic and romantic as that scene was, the message was not a very empowering one. I strongly believe that when we are complete within ourselves and feeling connected with our Higher Source, we have a much better chance at having healthy, loving, and fulfilling relationships with others. When we go into relationships and friendships feeling inadequate and expecting others to somehow fulfill our needs, and we are there to take care of their needs, it is very likely that the relationship will suffer. We are taught in relationships we need to compromise, and there is truth in that, but there is a big difference between compromise and sacrifice. Every individual must decide for themselves what they are comfortable giving without jeopardizing their own wellbeing. We need to respect and honor where our loved ones stand with this as well and take personal responsibility for our own happiness.

At this point in my life, I am no longer primarily focused on finding that "perfect person." I am more interested in being the best version of myself. I am finding that my relationship with my Higher Power is my primary focus and I let the rest of my life just unfold. I would love to meet someone to share my life with, but I am perfectly content if I never do. I totally understand that you may be in a very different place. Maybe you are wanting to start a family or just have a strong desire to be with someone, and that is perfectly fine. Just know that the more you develop your relationship with this Divine Energy or God or whatever you prefer calling it, the more you are going to enhance every relationship you have in your life.

Does my desire conflict with other goals and desires I have?

This can be a tricky one to decipher and sometimes we don't even realize that we have conflicting desires. I have found from personal experience that when I have a conflicting desire that I am not aware of, one sign is that my manifestations are off. If I feel I am doing my vibrational work and feel I am in alignment with my desire, then I may need to dig a little deeper to see why I am not attracting what I want. I just recently had an awakening of a conflicted desire that I have had for a very long time and did not even realize it.

For some time now I have wanted to be in a loving fulfilling relationship, but the ones I have attracted have been a little different from what I was hoping for. They weren't necessarily terrible relationships, in fact some were awesome love affairs, just not completely in alignment with my desires. After analyzing myself for some time I came to a realization. As much as I really wanted to be in a relationship, a part of me liked my independence and my personal space, and I would sometimes feel engulfed when I was in a relationship. I then started putting the pieces of the puzzle together. I really like having a lot of personal space, and I felt being in a serious relationship could be a threat to that, hence the conflicting desires. Once you get in touch with a contradictory desire you can start redirecting your energy accordingly. For me it was opening myself up to the belief that there was a man out there who would have similar desires and would be totally accepting of my need for personal space.

Is this desire about immediate gratification as opposed to long term fulfillment?

Desires are continuously being born throughout your day and it's important to examine and prioritize them to make sure they are not jeopardizing your future wellbeing or success. You will usually find that addictions fall into this area as well as financial debt. Credit card debt is a perfect example of satisfying the desire to have something now, and then paying huge amounts of interest to the banks and having nothing to show for it. Also, dieting is something we can all pretty much relate to. If we continue to overeat and make poor food choices, we will probably end up overweight and could be compromising our health as well.

It's the small choices you make every day that carve out the path to your future, and you just want to make sure they aren't sabotaging your heart's true desires. There is nothing wrong with indulging from time to time, but if you find it to be a pattern, you may want to look closer as to why you continue this behavior. Sometimes it can be a belief that we need to look at and we may need to adjust our energy around this area. The first step is being aware that acting on these desires is not in your highest interest, and then shift the energy to the greater vision you have for yourself and your life. In the chapters to follow, we will look at various ways to assist you in redirecting your energy and overcoming these types of challenges.

It is equally important to make sure you aren't sacrificing your present wellbeing and continuously "putting off" your present joy and happiness for some future time. Goals are important and we all want to feel like we have some direction in our life. Preparing yourself for a career, raising a family, mastering an art or sport all involve commitment and dedication. There are times in your life when it's appropriate to put the time and effort into accomplishing something you set out to do. These can be very rewarding and fulfilling experiences.

In our society, so many people work at jobs they hate because they have a good pension, or they plan to enjoy their life when they retire in twenty years. People will stay in extremely stressful jobs or relationships that are sucking the life out of them, which can lead to health challenges and all sorts of mental and emotional disorders. Most of the time when people stay in situations like this it's because they don't feel like they have choices, or they don't feel they have creative control in their lives. Life can be challenging at times, but we all have the power to make the changes we need to live more happy fulfilling lives if we choose to.

Is my desire trying to undo the past, or preventing something negative from happening in the future?

Old regrets or resentments can really block our creative

energy. We all have experiences in life that we wish would have turned out differently, and that's completely natural. But we can't go back and undo or change the past, so we need to get our energy focused on the future in a positive way. Sometimes before we can do this we need to forgive and forget old hurts and injuries. In fact, we may even be the person we need to forgive. It's important to acknowledge this, and then start taking steps immediately to let go these negative energy blocks. My mother use to always tell me, "It doesn't matter if you fell down the stairs, if you were pushed down the stairs, or if the stairway collapsed.......YOU are at the bottom of the stairs......What are YOU going to do about it?" Blaming others or yourself is giving your power away and leaves you feeling like a victim.

Revenge is another strong emotion that is related to blame. If someone has harmed you or a loved one it's very understandable that you might feel like blaming or getting revenge. Try not to judge yourself as you work through these feelings and urges. It is best to release these emotions in a productive way, since they are far more detrimental to you than the person or persons you are directing them toward. You may have heard the saying, "Resentment is like taking poison and waiting for someone else to die." When you are experiencing these emotions it's important to begin shifting the energy and taking your power back. There is a greater desire that was born from the experience. Maybe you want to attract different types of people or experiences, feel you can trust yourself and others, or overcome fears and release the past. The instant you start redirecting the energy and emotions in a positive way you will start to feel better, which in itself, is a manifestation which you can feel good about.

Worry is another unproductive energy that really robs you of enjoying and engaging in your life in the present moment. When you worry, you are actually projecting the past into the future because you are anticipating what might go wrong. Sometimes when we worry we believe that we are protecting ourselves, but this is just an illusion and has nothing to do with our present reality. If what you were worrying about was happening now, you would be reacting or responding to it now, as opposed to worrying or obsessing about it. The more we release fear and worry, the better and more able we are to respond to the challenge or circumstance in the present. When you get stuck thinking about the past or worrying about the future you are not living in present-time consciousness. And your power is always available to you in the present moment. The Law of Attraction is always responding to your current vibration. When you are focusing your energy on preventing bad things from happening or trying to protect yourself, that is your attraction point. This does not mean that you put you or your loved ones in compromising or harmful situations or bury your head in the sand, but it does involve shifting your energy in how you are perceiving yourself, and your experiences. See if you can "feel" the difference between these two statements.

"It's flu season and it seems every year I always catch something from someone at the office." Or "My body has a remarkable immune system and the more I have faith in its amazing abilities, the more I see it manifesting as health and wholeness in my body."

Both these statements may be true, but the latter is a far better place to focus your energy. You do not need to deny negative conditions or experiences, but it really doesn't do any good to give your power to them. Not to mention, the second statement "feels" so much better than the first. Over time, as you practice these principles, you will start to see changes occur in your life. First, you will genuinely feel better as you release pent up negative energy that you may not have even been aware you had. Next, you will start attracting experiences and people to reflect your new energetic setpoint back to you.

Is this desire a response to my ego and comparing myself to others?

Comparing yourself to others is a natural response and has value as it may increase your desire which in turn promotes expansion. However, sometimes we can feel inadequate and inferior by comparing ourselves to others, or we may feel superior and that others are beneath us. The reasons behind this can vary from wanting approval from others, having low self-esteem, or letting others define you as opposed to you defining yourself. When you feel resistance and negative emotions in your comparison, it's usually because you are pushing against what you don't want as opposed to saying 'yes' to what you do want.

For example, when you see someone who is very wealthy and spending their money in ways that you feel are frivolous, you may be feeling judgmental and possibly struggling with finances yourself. One way to transform this energy is to recognize that when they are circulating their wealth they are contributing to the abundance of others. You can also see yourself as financially abundant and spreading your wealth around. When you feel appreciation in your response to others, you raise your vibration and invite those qualities into your experience. We all have our own unique special gifts and when we are in a state of appreciation, we come into the fullness of who we are.

The only productive comparison that is truly relevant is where you currently are energetically, compared to the part of you that has expanded from your desire. In both observing and interacting with others you stimulate your desires. Then when you align your energy with the expanded desire, you raise your vibration and contribute to the expansion of all those you interact with.

Is my desire something I feel I 'should' do, or is it something I really 'want' to do?

We all have responsibilities and avoiding or neglecting them is certainly not going to bring you the happiness and fulfillment you seek. Legal and moral obligations are a part of life, so the first step would be to determine if the desire falls into these areas. As a parent, you have a moral obligation to your children, or you may have legal obligations that are punishable by law if not kept. Legal responsibilities are fairly easy to define. Moral ones can be tricky as belief systems can vary from individual to individual, so you will have to decide for yourself. In most cases, avoiding either one of these responsibilities can lead to grief and regret so accepting them is essential. If you feel overwhelmed it's important to find relief and release the pressure you are experiencing. I like to define responsibility as the ability to creatively respond to a situation. Do your best to release feeling burdened and focus your energy on attracting the appropriate resources to assist you in meeting your obligations. The most important thing you can do is transform the negative energy and create a new energy for the Law of Attraction to respond to.

I would say the majority of our "shoulds" are neither legal nor moral and are just desires we have been wanting to manifest in order to improve our lives, but we then tend to pressure or beat up on ourselves for them. I don't think you will ever hear anyone say, "I should have gotten really drunk last night and wasted my whole day sleeping away a hangover." Or "I should have cheated on my diet and gained weight." So, usually the intention behind the "should" is positive, since in truth, you want to be better or have better experiences. You want to release the feelings of struggle or resistance not the desire itself. Once you do this, you can replace the "should" with the feeling of joyful expectancy in its future manifestation.

A key factor to keep in mind is that whenever you are "shoulding" on yourself you are resisting the present moment, and until you make peace with the present moment you will always feel conflicted. You can only get to where you want to be in any area of your life by accepting your current circumstances. As long as you feel things should be different or you should be different, that is your vibrational setpoint, and you will continue to attract things to you that confirm this feeling of disapproval and dissatisfaction.

As you begin to work at the exercises in this book, don't feel you have to do it perfectly, just start somewhere. In time, it will get easier and you may even come up with your own exercises or modify those that I have given you. As you progress you will start to see your attraction point shifting with less and less "action" on your part, and more joy and fulfillment throughout your days.

Chapter Highlights

- Desire is the driving force behind all creation. It stimulates action which then produces new experiences and circumstances, which then new desires are born from.

- Desire is not something you have to search for or create, it is born out of your interaction with the world.

- Desires alone do not cause dissatisfaction or distress. It is your relationship with the desire that can cause feelings of inner conflict or power-lessness.

- The first step in transforming energy is to harmonize with your desire, and you do this by creating the essence of the desire.

- Evaluating desires is another important step to ensure you understand the pureness of the desire. There is a very distinct difference between understanding the purity of the desire as opposed to the lack of having it fulfilled.

- Some of our strongest desires can emerge from negative experiences. Do your best to release the negative experience and embrace the desire that evolved from it.

- Once you have a clear understanding of what you truly want, focus your energy and time on creating the new experience. Do so without pushing against the unwanted experience as this is the avenue where transformation begins.

CHAPTER 3

The Universal Field

Science without religion is lame; Religion without science is blind. --Albert Einstein

Science is the study of life. God is the creator of life. To know God is to study life. One of the ways to know God better is to study the physical world. Another way is to experience it through faith and love as well as our personal connection with this Divine Love. This chapter is about the science and philosophies that support the teachings in this book, as well as some of my personal beliefs.

I do not claim to be an expert in this field. This chapter is just a brief overview and there are many teachers out there if you would like to explore this information in more depth. If you are not comfortable with this information and feeling resistance that's fine too. It is not my intention to try and persuade or prove anything. In fact, I believe the best science is to prove it in your own life by applying the principles and techniques in this book. When I was first introduced to these teachings at the age of fourteen, I knew nothing about quantum physics and very little about the Law of Attraction, but when I started seeing things manifest in my world through the direction of my thoughts, that was enough proof for me.

To get a better understanding of what the Universal Field is we can explore the research of quantum physics, which studies the nature and behavior of matter and energy at the atomic and subatomic levels. Atoms are the building blocks of everything in the physical universe and although they appear to be 99.99 percent empty space, they are actually filled with energy frequencies which form an interconnected field of information. So, if all matter is made up of atoms, we can then presume that it is basically made up of energy and information. Upon examining the subatomic matter in the quantum field, scientists discovered it behaves differently than matter. It's very unpredictable and exists only as a tendency, probability, or a possibility, here one minute and then disappears the next. It was also discovered that when the particles of subatomic matter were being observed, it could affect or change the behavior. These two premises can lead us to believe that this field of energy and information is influenced by us and is filled with infinite creative potential.

Desire is the first ingredient in the Magic Potion and the Universal Field is the second. Once the desire is born it is released into the Universal Field of Infinite Possibilities, and what becomes of that desire will depend on how you nurture it. Think of it like planting a seed. This Universal Field is like the soil, and your thoughts, beliefs, emotions, and actions will determine how that desire unfolds. The Law of Attraction is in this field and is bringing to you those things that are in vibrational harmony with your dominant frequency, which is determined by your daily mental attitude, habitual thoughts, feelings, and beliefs.

Law of Attraction

The Law of Attraction is the magnetic power of the Universe. It's the creative medium that manifests through everyone and everything and it organizes the entire path from desire to fulfillment. It's like the Law of Gravity in that you can't see it and it's constantly working, regardless if you are consciously aware of it. It's based on the concept that like attracts like. Everything in the Universe is in a constant state of vibration and vibrations of similar frequencies are drawn together. This law is not something you decide to apply to your life, it is always working, so learning to manage your energy is essential in taking creative control in your life. The law is also an impersonal law, it's not good or bad it just is. Think of it like fire. It can either cook your food or burn down your house. It is not even necessary to understand the law, it is constantly responding to your energetic set-point and your only work is to become a vibrational match to what you want to attract in your life.

As you know, I started learning about the Law of

Attraction when I was a young girl. When people hear this they always say they wish they knew about this at such a young age, and how much better off they would be. I do feel very blessed to have been introduced to these teachings at such a young age, but keep in mind I still had the mind of a teenager, and most things I wanted were probably not for my highest good. So, I can personally attest that this law is impersonal, and like with fire, I sometimes got burned. I struggled with alcohol and drug abuse, was in an abusive relationship, and even attempted suicide. I obviously didn't understand the entire creative process at that time and was just beginning to learn all this, and I was clearly a troubled teenager to begin with.

Looking back, I think I was like most people when they first learn about these principles. I was really focusing on positive thoughts and doing affirmations as well as creative visualizations, but I didn't really have a firm grasp on managing my energy. Therefore, there were some areas of my life that were going great but others that were incredibly challenging. Despite all the trials and tribulations, I was a very determined and passionate young girl. I think the greatest thing I learned from these teachings is that I was not a victim, and I did have creative control in my life. I saw it manifesting in other areas as I was financially responsible and extremely ambitious, so that gave me the faith to keep trying and not lose hope.

Unlike a lot of other authors, I will not go into the details about the tough times I have been through and how I was able to rise above them. I realize that people like to feel that connection with someone who understands their pain and may have shared similar experiences, but that is the precise reason I am avoiding it. I want you to understand the most important lesson in this book, that by connecting to that energy you are continuing an energetic set point for the Law of Attraction to continue to respond to. Like I said, it's an impersonal law. It doesn't understand that you aren't currently having that experience, it only understands vibration, so there's really no value in me dragging you through the trenches of my past challenges and traumatic experiences.

When most people are first introduced to the Law of Attraction they learn about the power of positive thinking and that we are the creator of our experiences. Then, they look at their lives thinking, "I would have never created that!" or "How did this happen to me, when I wasn't thinking about that?" What most people don't re-alize is that taking creative control in your life is more than just trying to stay positive. Even though in that moment you may not have been consciously thinking about any-thing negative, we all have underlying vibrations in various areas of our lives. That is why it is so important to not only clear up negative energy you may be holding, but also to be very selective about what you are giving your attention to, as that will also influence your vibration as well.

The entire focus of this book is about transforming your energy so you can become a magnet for all the wonderful experiences you are wanting to manifest. That doesn't mean you will deny your feelings or avoid the circumstances you would like to be different in your life. It's impossible to never have a negative thought or feeling, and you don't want to get down on yourself when you are experiencing them, as that will create even more resistance. All your thoughts are not being created instantaneously, which allows you the time to evaluate them and shift your energy. Throughout this book I will be offering you exercises and techniques to assist you with learning how to become a vibrational match to what you would like to attract in your life.

Research Available to You

I would now like to offer some great studies and findings that are related to these teachings and some wonderful contemporary trailblazers who have paved the way in these fields. Their contributions to the study of The Mind Body Connection are significant and can assist in helping you to better understand this subject. These are just a few of the many resources out there, and I'm sure as you progress in these principles you will be introduced to many more. I personally enjoy exposing myself to this type of information as it helps me broaden my knowledge as well as solidify what I already know.

Bruce Lipton PhD

In 1970, Bruce Lipton, PhD, a stem cell biologist first introduced the idea that we are not pre-destined because of our genes. He discovered that by putting the same gene in a different petri dish, it would influence how the gene expressed itself. Twenty years later the study of epigenetics finally caught up with him. Most people still believe to this day that they are victims of their heredity and have no idea how our environment and our perception of it can greatly influence how a gene expresses itself. You have probably heard of the placebo effect. This is when a patient is given a sugar pill but is told it is a medication that will relieve the disorder they are experiencing, and because they believe it, it does. But there is also something referred to as the nocebo effect, which is when someone's negative thinking is equally as powerful and can create a disease. This breakthrough clearly shows that our bodies can be changed as we retrain our thinking.

The Energy of Water

Dr Masaru Emoto is a Japanese scientist who studied the scientific evidence of how the molecular structure in water changes when it is exposed to human words, thoughts, sounds and intentions. He was able to study this using Magnetic Resonance Analysis technology and high-speed photography. His research demonstrated that when water was exposed to loving, kindly and compassionate human intentions it formed beautiful molecular formations in the water, and that when water was exposed to fearful and discordant intentions the formations were disconnected and disfigured. He also studied how sound affected it and discovered that classical music produced beautiful crystalline patterns whereas heavy metal music produced ugly and distorted formations. If words, thoughts, sounds and intentions can do this to water just imagine what they can do to the human body that is about 70% water.

Joe Dispenza D.C.

Dr. Joe Dispenza, D.C. has been giving lectures and presenting workshops for years teaching others how to use the latest discoveries from neuroscience and quantum physics to reprogram their brains, heal illness, and lead more successful fulfilling lives. Part of his process is to feel the emotions of the future reality of the changed person you want to become, and to think and feel greater than your environment. One of his meditation processes starts by first becoming pure consciousness, which allows you to enter the invisible field of energy that unifies and connects everything material. Then you become clear with your intention and elevated emotion while you are in this state. He has measured the effects of this meditation using techniques such as brain mapping with EEG's to measure heart coherence to demonstrate the changes in his students. Dr Joes teachings have assisted many individuals in healing illness, as well as enjoying a more fulfilling and happy life.

Deepak Chopra M.D.

Deepak Chopra is a pioneer in integrative medicine and personal transformation and has written over 86 books. His first book, *Quantum Healing* was written in 1989. It combined western medicine, neuroscience, and physics as well as insights from Ayurvedic theory to demonstrate that the human body is controlled by a "network of intelligence" that is grounded in the quantum realm. He is a prominent figure in the original New Age movement and one of the most inspirational and influential spiritual teachers, authors, and thinkers of our time. Chopra has committed his life to uncovering knowledge that helps us connect to our highest good, mind, body, and soul. I have been following his work for 30 years and even have a book personally autographed by him from when I attended one if his meditation workshops. I will always treasure it as well as him and his teachings.

Heart Intelligence

The Heartmath Institute was founded in 1991 by Doc Childre. Traditionally the studies conducted in regard to the communication pathways between the brain and the heart primarily focused on the hearts response to the brains commands. We know now it is actually an ongoing two-way dialogue with each organ influencing the others function.

The heart is more than just an organ pumping blood, it is a complex information processing center with its own functioning brain that communicates with and influences the cranial brain, the nervous system, the hormonal system, and other pathways. When we experience uplifting emotions such as appreciation, joy, love, or compassion our heart rhythm patterns become highly ordered, looking like a smooth harmonious wave. This is called Heart Coherence and has been proven to improve your immune function, decrease stress hormones, improve heart health, and promote overall wellness.

Our Creator

The reason I used the heading Our Creator is because I believe God, or whatever word you prefer to use, is very personal to every individual. We are all unique, depending on where you were born, the faith you were raised in or what your life's journey has led you to believe. At this point in my life, I do not affiliate myself with any particular religion or faith. If someone asks me, I respond, "I am a student of life and a seeker of truth." As a student I am always growing, evolving and open to different views and philosophies, as well as striving to increase my under-standing of the All Knowing, All Powerful, All Loving, Divine Energy that is governing the Universe. The reason I do not associate myself with any one religion or faith is because I think that labels can sometimes build walls of separation and division, where I believe "Our Creator" is about unity and oneness. These are just my personal beliefs I am sharing, and I respect and honor every individuals right to their personal faith.

When we start studying this material it can start to feel very impersonal as science and laws are very factually based. But make no mistake, even though the Law of Attraction may be impersonal, our Creator is not. It is the Source of all Life and the Divine Intelligence and Love flowing through all creation. This Divine Love is the stabilizing force of all that is. At any moment we can choose to join with it or be separate, and in our separation is where we find negative emotions and thinking. When we are aligned with this All Loving Divine Energy, we are aligned with the higher part of ourselves. This Intelligence is what keeps the stars orbiting and our bodies functioning so precisely. Think about when you have a cut and need stitches. It's the body's intelligence that ultimately heals the wound. You do not need to know how to digest your food or create a baby inside you for these actions to take place. There is an underlying Intelligence governing all Creation, and even with man's greatest discoveries, we are just awakening to knowledge that already exists. We could have had computers and flown airplanes a thousand years ago; everything necessary to do so already existed, it was just waiting for us to realize it.

We are continually evolving, and expansion is a result of us being in this physical world. Diversity and choice are part of that expansion. As we are exposed to different things, we know what we want and don't want, and we all get to choose our preferences. Our Creator gave us the gift of free will and it's up to us to decide what we will choose. Are you choosing to line up with that All Loving, All Knowing, Greater Being, or are you choosing to line up with lack and limitation? Are you honoring everyone's right to choose, just like our Creator allows us the freedom to choose? Even if we don't agree with other people's choices, we can still honor their right to choose. Freedom and the power to choose are God's greatest gift to us and diversity is the premise of all expansion.

I like to feel we are a Spark of this Divine Energy. It's like this Universal Being is an ocean of water and we are like an individual wave. We come forth in this time and place personalized, and when we leave, it is as if we go back to the ocean. Everything that is inherent in the ocean is in every drop of water in the wave. God is the Creator of the Universe expressing through all that is, and we are the creator of our personal world. Throughout this book I refer to this Infinite Being in a multitude of names, and I encourage you to use whatever feels best to you. As far as I am concerned the name is irrelevant, it's how we are connected to this Divine Source of Love that really matters. The main objective of this book is to teach you how to establish that connection, and the tools and exercises offered will assist you in recognizing when you are resonating with this Divine Energy and when you are not. It's also important to understand that we are all connected with each other as well, coming from that same Source Energy that created all that is.

Chapter Highlights

- One of the ways to know God better is to study the physical world. Another way is to experience it through faith and love as well as our personal connection with this Divine Love.

- Atoms are the building blocks of everything in the physical universe and although they appear to be 99.99 percent empty space, they are actually filled with energy frequencies which form an inter-connected field of information. So, if all matter is made up of atoms, we can then presume that it is basically made up of energy and information.

- This field of energy and information is influenced by us and is filled with infinite creative potential.

- Once the desire is born it is released into the Universal Field of Infinite Possibilities, and what becomes of that desire will depend on how you nurture it.

- The Law of Attraction is in this field and is bringing to you those things that are in vibrational harmony with your dominant frequency, which is determined by your daily mental attitude, habitual thoughts, feelings, and beliefs.

- Everything in the Universe is in a constant state of vibration and vibrations of similar frequencies are drawn together.

- Even though the Law of Attraction may be impersonal, our Creator is not. It is the Source of all Life and the Divine Intelligence and Love flowing through all creation.

- There is an underlying Intelligence governing all creation and even with man's greatest discoveries, we are just awakening to knowledge that already exists.

- We are continually evolving, and expansion is a result of us being in this physical world.

- Freedom and the power to choose are God's greatest gift to us and diversity is the premise of all expansion.

CHAPTER 4

Thoughts

Whatsoever things are true, whatsoever things are honest,
whatsoever things are just, whatsoever things are pure,
whatsoever things are lovely, whatsoever things are of good
report, if there be any virtue, and if there be any praise, think
on these things. – Philippians 4:8

The next ingredient in the Magic Potion is our thoughts. Thoughts along with emotions, beliefs, and actions are where your creative control is. All of these have equal importance and thoughts tend to be the leader. When you have a thought, it releases a chemical that produces a corresponding feeling, such as anger, sadness, joy, fear, love, and the list goes on. And your thoughts generally precede your actions, so that is why thoughts are a great place to start the Creative Process. Keep in mind however what we reviewed in the previous chapter about heart coherence and that the heart is also sending messages to the brain. Over time we can become programmed by traumatic events, and we may find ourselves emotionally reacting to our environment. By intentionally creating feelings of well-being we can interrupt these patterns. So it really doesn't matter if you start with thoughts or emotions, as long as you start somewhere.

It has been estimated that our brains produce as many as 50,0000 thoughts per day, and unless you are a practiced meditator, your mind literally never shuts up. So, before we go into the effects your thoughts have on your experience, let's first get a better understanding of where thoughts reside. We all have a conscious and sub-conscious mind. The conscious mind represents about 10% of your brain's capacity where the other 90 % is sub-conscious. Your conscious mind is what most people associate with who you are and is how you communicate to the outside world. The subconscious mind is the store house of all memories and past experiences and from these your beliefs, habits and behaviors are formed. In this chapter we will primarily focus on using our conscious mind and in the chapter on beliefs we will focus on the sub-conscious mind.

The two most powerful functions of the conscious mind are its ability to direct your focus and its ability to imagine that which is not real. It's unrealistic to think that you can control every thought that comes to your mind, but you do have the ability to decide what thoughts you will give your attention and power to. An old saying my mother taught me was, "You may not be able to stop a bird from landing on your head, but you can certainly stop it from building a nest." Every thought we think is not creating our experience or our lives would be chaotic. Could you imagine if every thought materialized before your eyes? And yet it can't be denied the effect our thoughts do have on our experience.

The first thing a thought does is produce an emotional and physical response in your body. If someone upsets you, your emotional response may be anger and from that emotional response your body will start producing cortisone and your heart rate increases. If someone embarrasses you your face may turn red, and an ulcer is a perfect example of stress literally creating a hole in your stomach. The science is indisputable about the mind/body connection, and now with quantum physics we are starting to understand how our thoughts can affect our experience and environment. The attraction power of a thought is primarily determined by how often you have that thought and the feelings and emotions associated with it. The more energy you give to a thought the greater the attraction power. As we reviewed in the previous chapter the Law of Attraction is always bringing to you those things that are in vibrational harmony with your dominant frequency, which is determined by your daily mental attitude, habitual thoughts, feelings, and beliefs.

Let's first start with your ability to direct and focus your thoughts. It is important to understand that when you are directing your thoughts it is not your will or concentration that is doing the creating. Your will and concentration are not being used to compel or force something to happen, but rather allowing the stream of the Divine Energy in the Universe to take form. The will is only used in directing what you choose to focus on. Any idea of using the will to influence people or circumstances is a mistake, and that is why it is impossible for you to create in someone else's experience or for them to create in yours. The only way something can enter your experience is if you are a vibrational match to it. That is why it is so important to maintain a high frequency and not give your power away to negative thoughts and emotions.

Intention

Often, when we think of intention we think of determination or strong will, but as I stated earlier when you are directing your thoughts, you are not willing something to happen. You are releasing them to a force far greater than yourself and allowing it to flow into your experience. I like to think of intention as purpose or like a personal mission statement that we create as a general guide for the direction we want our life to take. You can have one main intention, or you may want to break it down into several of them for different areas of your life. Your intentions should be general and flexible and will most likely change throughout your life as the seasons of your life change. When you are raising a family, your intention may be to be a guiding loving force in your child's life. If you are wanting to express a creative talent it may be to share your gifts as a musician or artist. Or, if you are struggling with an addiction your main intention may be learning to love and honor yourself and allow your greatness to come forth to serve and benefit others.

Intentions are most powerful when they are about giving and serving. If your intentions are primarily to get something, then your dominant vibration is coming from a place of lack and need so that then becomes your attraction point. When your intention is to give, serve and share your gifts, you are sending off a much more powerful vibration and the Infinite Mind will respond to this point of attraction.

I currently have one main intention for my life and that is, "Living my life in a state of conscious connection with my Higher Power, sharing my unique and special gifts with wisdom and grace, and embracing the present moment with love and appreciation." This is my personal mission statement and I let it guide all my other desires and goals. If I have a specific desire I am looking to bring into my life, I will see how it relates to my main intention. It's like a compass that I can refer to making sure my actions are reflecting what's truly important to me and the direction I want my life to take.

For example, let's say I am considering a new job that would result in a significant increase in my income. I would first ask myself if I felt it would interfere with my conscious connection with my Higher Power. If it were a job that would be incredibly stressful or required me to work so many hours that it would interfere with my wellbeing, I may want to take a pass. Or maybe I have been finding myself being negative and judgmental about a situation or individual. "Embracing the present moment with love and appreciation" means focusing on the good and love all around me and feeling appreciation for the many blessings I am showered with. If I keep my choices and actions in line with my main intention, then I can be certain my life will be unfolding in fulfilling ways.

Now this doesn't mean that you may not have setbacks and struggles, that is totally natural and it's important that you don't get down on yourself. Sometimes in life we get off course, but the great thing about having a main intention is that you can more easily identify when you are off course and get back on track quicker. Self judgement and blame are a total waste of energy and you should do your best to avoid these lower vibrations. If you find yourself in these lower vibrations, you may want to evaluate some of your beliefs and see whether they may be contributing to you being so hard on yourself.

Clarity

Clarity is more specific than intention. It's really getting clear on the details and specific nature of your intentions and desires. A great way to gain clarity is to ask yourself, what you want and why you want it? How will your life look when you are living your new experience and how others will benefit, as well as how you will feel? Maybe you want to commit to once-a-week spending quality time with your children mentoring them or reading to them every night before they go to bed. Or having clarity with healing an addiction may mean regularly attending meetings and building a support group of like-minded people. If you are wanting to travel you may decide exactly where you would like to go, when, with who and for how long. When you want to gain clarity, you want to be as specific as possible filling in all the juicy details.

One important thing to remember when you are getting more specific is you want to make sure it feels good to you, and you are not feeling resistance. For example, you may have a goal to increase your income from making $50K a year to making $100k a year so you can have the funds to send your children through college. It's great to be specific but if this is creating feelings of stress and pressure you may want to adjust to something that feels more comfortable and believable like $70K a year as a first step. As you know, the Law is always responding to your vibration, so if you feel the goal you have set is highly unattainable then you want to adjust to thoughts that aren't creating resistance in you. You can always get more specific as you release the resistance. Sometimes the less specific you are, the more you feel at ease and in a state of allowing which gets the energy flowing. We will cover this concept more as we progress but it's particularly important to have a clear under-standing of it as it will have a powerful impact on your manifestations.

Your number one priority is to feel good and connected to your Source. That is when you are most powerful as you become a magnet for all good things to come into your experience. As you apply these different techniques you will see what works best for you and if you need to adjust. Your best bet is to feel your way through the experiences and be flexible in your approach. It's like having a toolbox and finding just the right tool you need at that moment. Sometimes a screwdriver is more appropriate than a hammer, only you can decide, and you may try several techniques until you feel a shift in energy. The main thing is don't give up or get discouraged. It may take some time to get familiar with some of this but once you do, I can assure you that you will start to see results.

Focus

Focus is about taking the time and putting the effort into these practices and disciplining yourself to keep your attention centered on what it is you are wanting to experience. This does not mean that you want to deny negative conditions or circumstances, but you do want to refrain from giving your attention to them. When you focus on the negative it usually creates feelings of powerlessness or dis-ease. These feelings only separate you from connecting to the All-Powerful, Divine Energy in the Universe and weaken you. You can never solve a problem or negative circumstance from the same consciousness or thought pattern that created it. You need to get your thoughts and energy focused on the solutions and creating a vision of what that looks like. This may seem hard at times, but it is really the best use of your energy, and you have so much more to contribute when you are coming from a place of connection with your Higher Power.

There will be times in your life when you are confronted with situations, experiences, and people that you would like to be different. If what you are observing is bothering you, it's not effective to pretend that it doesn't. You certainly need to acknowledge what you are feeling and honor your desire to have a better experience. But it's not productive to give your power away by complaining or pushing against the conditions or people that you are not pleased with. It's far more productive to define what it is you want to experience, what you would like your relationships to look like, and then direct your focus on those outcomes.

As we reviewed earlier, the two most powerful functions of the conscious mind are its ability to direct your focus and its ability to imagine that which is not real. There are many techniques that will assist you in this and I suggest you sample with as many as possible to find which ones resonate with you. And you may want to try different ones for different circumstances. There is no right or wrong, the main thing is that you are taking the time to practice and doing your best to direct your thoughts. I like to compare it to Yoga, there is the philosophy behind it and its practice. Of course you need to have the knowledge, but just reading about it and going to lectures is not going to have much of an impact in your life. You must take the time daily to practice and master the postures and breathing, that is when you will start to see the changes in your body and well-being.

Affirmations

To merely refrain from negative thoughts is not enough, you must construct new thoughts and new ideas. Affirmations are one powerful way of directing your thoughts and a very simple place to start. I was first introduced to affirmations in the early 1980's at a New Thought Spiritual Center I was attending, and they called it affirmative prayer. The center also had a book called, *You Can Heal Your Life,* by Louise Hay, who in my opinion was the Queen of Affirmations. If you are not familiar with her work, I highly recommend it. She was a pioneer in mental and emotional equivalents to physical ailments, as well as using affirmations for healing and well-being. To this day, anytime I have any kind of health challenge I always refer to her book to gain insight and always find it immensely helpful and enlightening.

When using affirmations there are three guidelines that will help you achieve the best results. First, you must say the affirmation out loud. Reading it may be beneficial but not nearly as powerful as speaking it out loud with conviction and passion. There is something about hearing yourself speak these words that helps them penetrate. Remember you are not trying to make or force anything to happen, your main objective is to change your thinking and feelings on the subject and clear up any negative energy you may have. Another powerful action is refraining from saying something negative, complaining or gossiping. There will be times when you have negative thoughts, but not fueling them with your energy and word is beneficial and can lessen their impact greatly.

Second, you should always speak them in the present tense and not project something into the future. Even though it may be regarding a future event, you are wanting to change your vibration on the subject in the present moment as that is always where your power is. For example, say you are planning a vacation in the future but want to set an intention now as to how you want to experience it. You might say "I now see myself having a fabulous time on my trip enjoying perfect weather and sharing it with fun loving spirits." Affirmations are not for the purpose of willing something to happen, but they do provide within you an avenue for things to happen. They expand your consciousness by removing doubt and fear and open your mind to infinite possibilities.

Lastly, the most crucial thing about an affirmation is you must believe what you are affirming. To make positive statements that you don't feel are true or have any conviction behind them is not going to have much impact on your experience. Your belief in what you are affirming is what is fueling its creative potential. The best way to determine how effective your affirmation is going to be is to see how it feels. For example, if you say, "I am experiencing perfect health and I feel great" and at the moment you feel rotten because you have a terrible cold, you will most likely not feel a lot of conviction behind your affirmation. However, if you say something like, "The Divine Life Force in the Universe is now permeating through every cell of my body returning it to the perfection it originated from." then you may have a more positive response. Only you can determine how an affirmation feels to you, so you may need to tweak it a bit to find one that resonates with you. A successful affirmation will uncover, neutralize, and erase false images of thought and replace it with positive statements of truth.

A lead into an affirmation that I sometimes like to start with is, "I'm ready." It's really a great indicator to see if you are a vibrational match to what it is you want. I recall one time in the past saying, "I am now ready for my right and perfect mate to come into my experience" and immediately I felt uneasy and doubtful. I instantly knew I had to explore why I was having these feelings and do some more energy work. In the meantime I found an affirmation that didn't bring up any tension which was, "I am willing to be open to meeting my right and perfect partner." This felt so much better to me and was a great transition affirmation until I could state the first one without any resistance.

The following are some examples of what I call lead into the affirmations for you to sample and see how it "feels" when you state them. Sometimes you may need to ease your way from softer declarations to more powerful ones.

I am in the process of learning

I am in the process of healing

I am open to guidance

I now accept my guidance

I am loving myself through this process

I love knowing

I am willing to change

I open my mind and heart

I am willing to let go

I now choose to change

I'm starting to see myself in a new light

I am now releasing

I am enjoying the process

I am finding it easier

I like the new idea of myself I am creating

I am excited about

I am willing to see this situation differently

I choose to focus on

I am enjoying the transformation

I am enjoying the journey

Everyday gets easier and easier

I am on my way

I am happy with the progress I am making

I am learning to trust myself

I am ready

Changing Your Perspective

Another way to direct your thoughts is to change your perspective. Our perspective is the way we view or interpret something, and there are certainly many ways to look at the experiences and people in our lives. I'm sure you heard the saying, "Is the glass half empty or half full?" or "When you change the way you look at things, the things you look at change." You always have a choice as to how you want to perceive the positive or negative experiences in your life, and how you choose to look at them can greatly impact your life. If you are constantly seeing yourself as a victim, I can almost guarantee that you are probably continuing to attract people and experiences to reaffirm this belief you have. Or you can decide to look at life as a classroom, always bringing you experiences to grow and evolve. This is a far more empowering way of looking at things, and if your intention is to learn and grow you will continue to progress in a positive direction.

One technique you can try is what I call "Looking Forward." So many of us spend much of our time either observing and reacting to the present moment or rehashing the past. This can be very beneficial if what you are observing or remembering is pleasing to you, but unfortunately that may not be the case. If you are not feeling good about an experience or situation you find yourself in, start by writing a paragraph or so about what has happened and why it is upsetting to you and what feelings or emotions you are feeling. Then you want to ask yourself, "What desire was born from this?" This is a great way to shift your attention from what is and focus your energy on how you would like to feel and how this experience could be improved or changed going forward. By doing this you are no longer pushing against or struggling with what is. You are now directing your focus to creating your future experiences and starting to envision what that might look like.

Another way of changing your perspective is by evaluating what has happened and what you can learn from it. Experiences can create an opportunity for you to stand from a different vantage point. If you have attracted an experience in your life it is there for a reason, and if it's not for your joy then it's for your growth. A great question to ask yourself is, "What kind of belief could create something like this? This is not to create feelings of guilt or blame, but to objectively analyze if there is a false belief you are now ready to release. We will cover beliefs in another chapter, but for the purpose of changing your perspective it is helpful to understand if a false belief is limiting you in any way. Or maybe you can look at the experience and see how much you have grown and changed and praise yourself for the progress you are making. Learning and evolving are very positive energies, and this is a very productive practice in redirecting negative thoughts and energy.

Beholding the best for others is a great tool to use in your relationships, especially if you are having challenges with certain individuals in your life. Sometimes people have certain personality traits that you might find very frustrating, even our dearest loved ones get off course or do things that we may find very annoying. Obviously, you want to stay focused on their positive qualities and appreciate the good they add to your life. When you behold the best for others, you go one step further and not only focus on the good in them but also see them living to their fullest potential. As opposed to giving your attention to what they may be living out in the moment, you see them living their lives in joy and love expressing what they most hold dear in their hearts. There is no better gift you can give to another than to acknowledge the greatness in them and see them flourishing. You can also quickly change your perspective by looking at what you can give to a relationship or situation as opposed to what you can get, or how it is affecting you. You will be amazed when you try these practices and see the positive effects that they will have on you and your relationships.

Trying to see the broader perspective is another great way to direct your thoughts. There is an old saying, "You can't see the forest through the trees." Sometimes when you are involved in an experience, you can get caught up in emotions and the details of it and lose site of the overall big picture. It can be helpful to take a step back and distance yourself from the situation and your emotional attachment. The song From a Distance that was released in 1990 beautifully illustrates this. I will sometimes ask myself the question, "How would God see this?" This powerful question can really have a dramatic impact on your perceptions.

These are just a few examples of ways to keep a positive outlook and release undesirable energy. You will know if your perspective has changed if you can stand in the negative experience or look at it and know All is Well. The resistance around the subject will be released and you will feel peaceful and at ease.

Imagination

Imagination is another powerful tool to use in taking creative control of your life and it can be a lot of fun. Albert Einstein said, "Imagination is more important than knowledge. For knowledge is limited, whereas imagination embraces the entire world, stimulating progress, giving birth to evolution." Imagination frees our mind and allows us to expand our concepts of what's possible for us. Visualization is one way to use your imagination to create a clear mental image of that which you want to manifest. When you create the image of the experience or thing you want to attract in your life, it's like forming a mold for the Divine Energy to take form. It's one of the easiest ways to create change in your life and it's relatively effortless, you just need to make the time for it.

One of my favorite forms of visualization are vision boards, I have one that is almost twenty years old and I still use it today. I like to pull out my boards and look at them while I'm walking on my treadmill or riding my stationary bike, it's a great way to allow time for it with my busy schedule. I have different themes for them such as a health and well-being board, a relationship board, and a physical fitness board. I also have binders that I save pictures that resonate with me, and I still have the one I made when I was looking for a home. I periodically look back at that binder as a reminder of how powerful this tool is and how much my home resembles the images in that binder.

The first thing you want to do is start gathering images of things or experiences you want to bring into your life, or even just an image that you gravitate to. For example, I once clipped a picture of a cat lifting its head up with its eyes closed just basking in the sunshine. To me it was a symbol of taking in the present moment and just allowing what is to be. It's on my health and well-being board and to this day I still visualize that image. My relationship board is filled with pictures of couples doing fun things together and really captures the spirit of the ideal relationship for me. You can also have words that describe the way you want to feel in the experience such as "Love-Cherish-Free-Passion-Adventure-Easy-Fun." The most important thing to keep in mind is that you want to create a feeling that coincides with the image. This really ignites the creative forces in the Universe and raises your vibration making you a magnet for your good.

I also have index cards that pertain to different areas of my life such as health, career, prosperity, relationships, spirituality, and travel. On each card I write my intention for that area in my life, and the images I refer to that reflect that intention. I then write a caption of how that image feels to me or how I want to feel in the experience. For example, my prosperity intention is "I cocreate a life filled with unlimited abundance. I welcome infinite possibilities and allow good to flow to me and through me, manifesting my desires with ease and grace. I live in a state of joyful expectancy, feeling love and appreciation for my magnificent life." One of the images I refer to is a girl on a swing and my feeling is "Carefree." Another is an old greeting card with an image of a dog hanging his head outside a car window with the wind blowing in his face and the feeling is "Enjoy the ride." I have one of a girl walking with numerous shopping bags in her hands with the caption "Circulation." And another of a girl walking the beach and the sensation I felt looking at it was "Surrendering to the unknown." As you see not one of my images was a material object or anything really specific, but the emotions and feelings generated were very precise. This is comparable to creating the essence of the desire that we previously reviewed and is an extremely potent technique. The great thing about this technique is that it is not as specific as harmonizing with your desire. Sometimes when we are less detailed and just focus on the emotions we don't have as much resistance, as we work on raising our vibration.

Another imagination technique you can try is Creative Visioning. This differs from the previous as instead of just an image, you envision an entire experience. You can apply this to numerous areas of your life such as overcoming a bad habit or something you feel may be inhibiting you, or for planning a future event. You can also use it to create visions for different areas of your life, such as health, relationships, career, creative self-expression, prosperity, and spirituality. The list is endless. When you create a vision, you describe and see yourself in the experience you want to create. It's not necessary when you do this to actually see an image, although some people do. You may just be thinking about it, describing the details, or getting a feeling or a sense of what it would be like.

I like to do this in the morning while I'm lying in bed after I wake up or just before I fall asleep at night. It's so fun and relaxing, and I really look forward to it every day. This morning I worked on overcoming a behavior I would like to change. I tend to eat very quickly, always in a rush and don't take the time to chew my food thoroughly. So, I took about five minutes to imagine when I'm eating taking my time, feeling relaxed, being present, giving thanks, and really enjoying every bite. Sometimes I still do it unconsciously, but now I become aware of it almost immediately so I can change my behavior. This can be a highly effective tool in releasing unwanted habits and creating new positive behaviors.

Another area this could be useful is if there is a person you find difficult to deal with or someone who really gets you off center. Write out how you want to feel in their presence and how you want to handle irritations or conflicts. Then see yourself being that person you want to be in that experience. Calm, centered, and confident. Maybe you can respond by taking a few deep breaths or politely excusing yourself so you can take some time to regain your composure. It's like a rehearsal, preparing yourself for how you want to respond to different circumstances in your life.

My favorite Creative Visioning is imagining a future event, and a great place to start is with your physical senses such as site, taste, touch, scent, and sound. I had mentioned earlier in this book that my first major demonstration was a car when I was sixteen. When I was fourteen and fifteen, as I rode my bike, I would imagine that I was driving my car. I would see myself driving with my windows down, feeling the wind on my face, and listening to my favorite music. Another vision I am working on right now is imagining an upcoming vacation I have planned. For this I wrote a detailed description of all the details that are important to me such as the weather, accommodations, fun activities, as well as travel arrangements. I will periodically refer to it prior to my trip just to reinforce it. This is what it looked like:

"I now see myself enjoying a fabulous vacation. I have wanted to come here for such a long time and it's everything I dreamed it would be. All our flights and travel arrangements are all on schedule and flowing smoothly. Mary is such a great traveling companion, and we enjoy each other's company so much. The weather is perfect for enjoying outdoor activities and sightseeing. There are so many awesome affordable restaurants to choose from with delicious food and a beautiful atmosphere. The Riverwalk is spectacular with many unique shops and attractions. The wine country is so picturesque and has so many quaint wineries to visit with excellent wine selections.

All the clothing I packed is perfect for the weather and exactly right for all our activities. It's such a fabulous trip, the perfect balance between activities and relaxation. Our accommodations are clean, comfortable, and peaceful and all the people we meet are friendly, fun loving spirits. We are creating so many happy memories and embracing every moment with love, joy and appreciation."

These are just a few examples of ways to utilize your imagination, you may come up with other techniques on your own. I highly recommend dedicating time every day to some form of visualization along with affirmations. These are great tools in directing your thoughts and once you start to see the impact they can have on your life, you will want to make them part of your daily practice.

Chapter Highlights

- Thoughts are a great place for you to start as they tend to produce your emotions and precede your actions.

- The conscious mind represents about 10% of your brains capacity and the other 90 % is sub conscious.

- The two most powerful functions of the conscious mind are its ability to direct your focus and its ability to imagine that which is not real.

- It's unrealistic to think that you can control every thought that comes to your mind, but you do have the ability to decide what thoughts you will give your attention and power to.

- The attraction power of a thought is primarily determined by how often you have that thought and the feelings and emotions associated with it.

- Your will and concentration are not being used to compel or force something to happen, but rather allowing the stream of Divine Energy in the Universe to take form.

- When you have an intention to give, serve and share your gifts, you are sending off a powerful vibration and the Infinite Mind will respond to this point of attraction.

- Clarity is really getting clear on the details and specific nature of your intentions and desires. When you are getting more specific make sure it feels good to you and you are not feeling resistance.

- Focus is about taking the time and putting the effort into these practices. It's important to keep your attention centered on what it is you are wanting to experience.

- You can never solve a problem or negative circumstance from the same consciousness and thought patterns that created it.

- To merely refrain from negative thought is not enough, you must construct new thoughts and new ideas. Affirmations are a powerful and simple place to start.

- Affirmations are not for the purpose of willing something to happen, but they do provide within you an avenue for things to happen. They expand your consciousness by removing doubt and fear and open your mind to infinite possibilities.

- Another way to direct your thoughts is to change your perspective. Our perspective is the way we view or interpret something and there are certainly many ways to look at the experiences and people in our lives.

- Imagination is another powerful tool to use in taking creative control of your life. Imagination frees your mind and allows you to expand your concepts of what's possible for you.

- Visualization is one way to use your imagination to create a clear mental image of that which you want to manifest.

- When you create the image of the experience or thing you want to attract in your life, it's like forming a mold for the universal stuff to take form.

- The most important thing to keep in mind is that you want to create a feeling that coincides with the image. This really ignites the creative forces in the Universe and raises your vibration making you a magnet for your good.

CHAPTER 5
Emotions

Pain is inevitable. Suffering is optional. --Haruki
Murakami

Your emotions are another ingredient in the Magic Potion and are what's fueling The Creative Process. Your emotions are an indicator of where you are vibrating on various subjects and what the Law of Attraction is responding to. Your emotions can tell you whether you are lining up with the essence of your desire or the lack of it. Too often the importance of our emotions are overlooked as we focus on positive thinking, and this was something I didn't totally grasp until I was in my forties. I would practice saying my positive affirmations, worked on limiting beliefs, and visualized my desires, but then spend the rest of my day emotionally reacting to people and circumstances. I still had some wonderful manifestations, but when I really grasped this concept it was like the flood gates opened and I really started having major shifts in all areas of my life. When I discovered the teachings of Abraham Hicks and the emotional scale it really pulled it all together for me in a very profound way. The emotional scale is a great tool as it illustrates the progression from negative emotions to positive and can assist you with identifying where you are on the scale, as well as the progression you want to make. There are several versions of it available online and I highly recommend getting yourself familiar with it.

I must admit, when I was first introduced to the teachings of Abraham, I was skeptical. The whole idea of someone channeling this non-physical energy seemed a little farfetched to me. It wasn't until I lost my first dog Ebony that I really opened up and started comprehending it more deeply. I was in such terrible grief and I was having a very difficult time dealing with it. I had always been a happy person, but losing Ebony caused me to experience a tremendous sense of emptiness and loss, and I wanted so much to ease the discomfort. I started purchasing the Abraham DVD's and when I saw Abraham (Ester Hicks) in action my skepticism faded. The teachings really helped me in moving through my grief and expanding my understanding of the Law of Attraction and what an important role our emotions play. Even our negative emotions serve a purpose. And the wonderful thing about emotions is we can learn to use them as a guide to let us know where our current attraction point is.

There are several challenges you may experience when trying to move up the emotional scale. One is feeling bad about having the negative emotions, which keeps you stuck in the negative energy and creates a vicious circle. Another is trying to go from a very negative emotion to a very positive one, which can lead to frustration when you are unable to make a huge shift too quickly. This is why the emotional scale is so beneficial as even the slightest progress can bring a feeling of relief, which is very beneficial if you are in a very negative state. If you find yourself feeling critical of how you are feeling it's important to realize that your emotions are not a reflection of who you are, they are just a reflection of your energetic set point. Most of the time they are programed responses that have been engraved in us for years. It's not necessary to always be in a state of complete joy, and it's unrealistic to think you should be. The main goal is to ease any tension and then direct your focus to areas that you enjoy.

Anger the Doorway to Empowerment

We are all familiar with feeling angry, yet we all have different ways of dealing with or expressing our anger. How you were raised will have a huge impact of how you manage anger, and societal expectations influence us as well. In general, expressing anger is usually viewed as inappropriate and because of this we have learned to shut down our anger. Women especially are judged much differently than men when it comes to expressing anger. Women can be labeled as difficult or bitchy, whereas men are perceived as tough and powerful. Even though there can be a lot of stigma attached to anger, it can really serve us if understood and directed appropriately. My mother raised me and my brothers to express our anger freely. She was a single mom and knew she could not always be there to protect us and understood that our anger would. And although my temper has sometimes created problems for me as an adult, I am still grateful to my mother for recognizing that all our emotions serve a purpose.

When looking at the emotional scale there are many labels for the different emotions, but it's basically a path from disempowerment to empowerment, and anger is the point where you can begin to take your power back. When you are in a state of depression, guilt, unworthiness, or feeling victimized you feel powerless and weak. Getting angry is the first step toward regaining your power and you can literally feel this as the cortisol floods through your body and the fight or flight response kicks in. If you suppress your anger when you begin to experience it, you are just pushing yourself back into a state of disempowerment. If you have difficulty experiencing your anger it can be that you are concerned about what others will think, or how they will respond to your anger. Or when you do express it, you may feel guilty, or embarrassed which puts you back into a state of disempowerment.

I am in no way suggesting that you want to feed your anger or act out destructively. It's very important to work through these negative emotions as soon as you can. There is a difference between feeling your anger and expressing it in productive ways, as opposed to suppressing it or striking out. We do this first by honoring how we feel, expressing it constructively, and then utilizing it to shift to more positive emotions. We can't usually go from very negative states to joy and bliss instantaneously, and we also can't just keep saying positive affirmations when inside we feel very differently. I have worked with the following exercises and found them extremely helpful in defusing negative energy and transforming it in a new direction.

The Emotional Release and Sooth and Uplift Letters

One effective way to work through your negative emotions is by using the Emotional Release Letter (ERL). Affirmations and changing your focus are great ways to stop momentum from building in the present, but some situations may need a little more effort. If you are presently experiencing intense emotions, or it's an area you find yourself struggling with often, you may find this helpful. The purpose of the ERL is to release the emotional tension and then begin to redirect your energy in a more positive way. If you don't transform your negative energy your energetic set point will remain where you last left it, so it's very important to make this effort. It's futile to just proclaim positive affirmations if they are not providing you with a shift in your energy. They are just empty words and of very little benefit.

It's a very simple exercise and can sometimes bring immediate relief if you are experiencing anger, anxiety, depression, or any feelings of powerlessness. All you need to do is just write out exactly what is bothering you and how you feel about it. This is not a time to monitor what you are saying. You don't need to be objective or worry about hurting anyone's feelings. You just want to let it all out unfiltered and allow it to flow spontaneously, getting all your thoughts and emotions out there to evaluate. Emotions can be tricky to decipher and through this process you will often reveal blocks or limiting beliefs you may not even be aware of. For example, one time I was writing an ERL because I was frustrated with a person who I felt was constantly complaining. Through the process, I discovered that one of the reasons I was feeling bad was because I could not make this person happy. I was not consciously aware that I was feeling responsible for their happiness, which was a big part of my frustration. Sometimes writing a letter to the person can release tension as well, but not with the intention of giving it to them. The purpose of this exercise is to shift your energy, not change anyone else's behavior or point of view.

The next step is the Sooth and Uplift Letter (SUL) which is intended to comfort you and begin to neutralize the negative energy. You can write this immediately after finishing the ERL or give yourself a little time to assimilate what was revealed. When I'm writing the SUL, I like to think it's my higher self or my Higher Power writing the letter to me personally in response to my difficulty. The main goal of the SUL is to ease the tension you are experiencing, not to fix the situation or the person you are having the conflict with. You are not trying to figure out how it will be resolved, when it will happen, how it will come to you, or the final outcome you may desire. It's all about making yourself feel better like a comforting friend would do, and then raising your vibration from the negative state you were in. It's not necessary that you feel complete joy or empowerment as long as you get a feeling of relief from whatever was bothering you.

After you write the letters try to determine what desire was born from this situation, and why you want it. This will offer you guidance when you are ready to re-direct your energy. Here is an example of an ERL and SUL letter that I wrote to give you a feel for what this process looks like. I am using the example of a complaining friend (changed the name) that was really starting to sap my energy.

Sample ERL Letter

I'm so tired of listening to Barb complain and whine. That's all she does, and the things that she is complaining about are so irrational. A part of me feels bad because I am getting impatient, but then another part of me feels she is very self-absorbed to continually dump all her negative energy on me. I'm starting to feel resentful. And when I try to uplift her, she just makes all these excuses and complains even more. She doesn't want to solve her problems she just wants to bitch. I don't like feeling responsible for her and it's very upsetting to me because I want to see her be happy. I feel bad because no matter how much I try to assist her, she never wants to even try to solve her problems.

Sample SUL Letter

Dear Gina,

I know she's a difficult person to deal with at times and I can see why you are having these negative feelings. Try not to be so hard on yourself. I know how much you care about your friend and want to be supportive. I know it's important for you to be a positive influence in her life and see her be happy. Unfortunately, you cannot make her happy so just do your best to let her be. The main reason you get so upset is because somehow you feel responsible. I think it would help a lot if you just let yourself and her off the hook. She is doing her best and you are doing your best, and you both love each other very much. She has her own Higher Power and internal guidance and is very capable of solving her own problems. The best thing you can do for her is maintain your own energy alignment, honor your spirit, and be a positive loving example in her life.

The beginning of the SUL was aimed at quieting that internal critical voice that was judging me for having the negative emotions. You can see from the ERL I was feeling guilty and frustrated that I could not uplift my friend. Because of this awareness I was able to relieve myself of feeling responsible for someone else's happiness, which was one of the main reasons for my frustration. It's important that feel your way through these exercises and leave yourself open to where they may take you. I also did not try to change the behaviors or actions of anyone. Everything was directed at me and how I could change or see the situation differently. The main goal of the SUL is to provide a feeling of relief from the tension you are feeling. Once you have accomplished that you are ready to start transforming the energy and move forward to outlining your desires more specifically. Here is an example of a reframing affirmative prayer that started getting my energy moving in a more positive direction.

Sample Reframing Affirmation Prayer

I now choose to release Barb from any expectations and free myself from any negative thoughts or feelings about her. People come into our lives for all sorts of reasons and I do see the value in our relationship. I like that I am getting better at maintaining my positive energy in my relationships. It feels so freeing to separate my energy from others and remain centered and grounded. As I allow others the freedom to experience their life however they choose, I give myself the space to feel and honor my own feelings. I release any conflicts to our Creator who adores both of us.

Another way of re-directing your energy is to affirm what is going right in a situation. We sometimes tend to focus on the negative and a shift in perspective can help us stay centered on the positive things going on. Here is an example of an affirmation I wrote while experiencing some health challenges. Keep in mind I wrote this after an ERL, and SUL and I felt my energy was in a more neutral place.

1. It's awesome that I have not had a cold or flu bug in years.

2. I'm also so pleased with how quickly my body healed from my recent injury.

3. It feels so great to be able to work out on a consistent basis and be so athletic.

4. I love that I can enjoy long walks with my dog and on my treadmill.

5. I am so grateful my body has given me so many years of health and vitality to enjoy this fabulous life.

6. I like knowing that my heart and lungs are in phenomenal shape.

7. It's great that my digestion has been improving every day.

8. I have faith I will be guided in any action I need to take through this healing process.

9. I believe with every fiber of my being that "With God all things are possible" and I can be healed.

10. I'm so happy I know about the Law of Attraction and have a solid understanding of these principles.

11. I believe in my ability to transform my energy and like knowing that the Law will respond.

12. I love my body and getting good at knowing what it needs to thrive.

13. It's so reassuring to know that the Universe totally supports me in providing whatever is necessary for my body to have a complete and total healing.

14. I am ready to be completely healed.

15. I am ready to thrive.

You may be tempted to put off or avoid doing these exercises because of the time and effort involved, but I can assure you it's well worth it. I may sometimes wait a day in between letters, but I always make sure I get the energy flowing in a positive direction. I will then continue to read the affirmative prayer numerous times until I feel it sinking in, and this may take some time. Sometimes I even go back to the SUL if I am feeling discouraged. You are clearing negative energy and creating new thought patterns so be patient with yourself. Affirmations and creative visualization are great tools, but it's like painting over chipped paint if you don't release the negative energy first. If you have done this exercise properly you will feel a shift in energy. You don't have to be in Joy and Passion, but you do want to feel some relief and separation from the negative emotions you were experiencing. The more you do this the better you will get at it and you will begin to experience remarkable results.

Quick Fix

I realize life can get hectic, so I want to offer a quick easy technique to use with emotions that can help to diffuse the energy in the moment. When you start to feel the anxiety, anger, fear or hurt say out loud, "I acknowledge you and I honor you, but I choose _____instead. You can fill that blank in with whatever you want:

- I choose peace.

- I choose love.

- I choose freedom.

- I choose to line up with the greater part of me.

- I choose to direct my energy to the future.

- I choose to learn and grow from this experience.

- I choose to look for the good.

- I choose to transform my energy.

- I choose to do what's best for me.

- I choose prosperity and abundance.

- I choose radiant health.

This will assist you in breaking these emotional response patterns. Remember to always start with, "I acknowledge you and I honor you." Then take a moment to feel where it is in your body. Our emotions play an important role in our wellbeing and they want your attention. Your intent is to transform the energy, not suppress it. You still may need to write an ERL if the pattern continues, but at least you will start the process of weakening these conditioned responses and guiding your energy in a positive direction.

Another way to quickly release emotional tension is to have a good cry. This physical release can be very beneficial. When you cry you are releasing toxins and hormones that can cause elevated stress levels, and it can really have a calming effect. It's very common when you progress in managing your energy you become less tolerant of negative emotions and may also feel guilty expressing sadness and allowing yourself this type of release. I recently had a situation that upset me so much I was literally sobbing. I had not cried in years and had not cried in this manner for almost ten years, but I just allowed myself to get "unhinged". This had been building up for a long time and it took over me completely. Initially I tried to resist it, but once I started I could not stop. Afterwards I felt so peaceful, calm, and relaxed. It totally cleared my mind from the negative rampage I had been on and I was now open to creative solutions. I could feel a complete shift in my energy, so I knew it was effective.

Fine Tuning Your Energetic Setpoint

As you progress with these exercises and techniques

you will discover that you are much more in tune with your emotions than you previously were, and you will become less tolerant of negative emotions. Fine tuning is taking it to the next level and really paying close attention to precisely how you are feeling. These subtle energetic shifts can be extremely powerful. For example, feel the difference between Acceptance and Allowing. Which feels less resistance? Acceptance can feel like having to settle or tolerate something whereas allowing can feel more like you are agreeing or permitting something. Acceptance can certainly feel more positive than frustration, regret, or blame, but may still need a little tweaking. Keep in mind the actual word being used is irrelevant, what matters most is how it feels to you. With these examples, I am just trying to illustrate the slight variations of vibration. Another comparison is Motivation verses Inspiration. Obviously, motivation feels better than feeling listless, but motivation can have a feeling of pushing yourself to do something you really don't want to do. Whereas, inspiration can feel more like an urge, where you are being drawn to something or a creative impulse. Have you ever felt like you really deserved something? It can feel like strongly wanting for something you are not getting or having a feeling of entitlement. I like the word worth better. To me if feels like being of value "I am worthy of this", as opposed to "I deserve this."

"Protection" is another word I hear used a lot, especially when people are feeling vulnerable and they are praying for protection. Feeling protected is far better than feeling fearful or worried about something, but it tends to have a feeling of needing to be protected from something underlying it. Try substituting "feeling loved and provided for" instead and see how that feels. When you feel loved and all your needs are provided for you will inevitably feel protected. Or how often do you hear people say, "I am a cancer survivor." How about being a "Post cancer thriver" Are you looking for friends who will be supportive or a support group? Or do you want to be surrounded by people who empower and inspire you? This is not about judgement or thinking one emotion is superior to the other. If you were feeling rejected and alienated it may feel very nice to have loving supportive people around. But if you are using them as an avenue to reinforce your negative emotions and sad stories, then that is something you might want to look at. This may seem silly, or like we are splitting hairs, but keep in mind that the Law of Attraction is always responding to your energetic set point. Learning to "feel" these differences will really assist you in fine-tuning your energy and becoming more sensitive to subtle vibrations. I have personally experienced phenomenal results when I make these subtle shifts.

Empaths

I want to touch briefly on Empaths as they can really benefit greatly from this type of energy management. I discovered I was an empath about five years ago and it was a major awakening. When I first became aware of the traits it was like someone describing me better than I could myself. I had no idea there was a "label" for it, and other people out there like me. In a way it was comforting because I always felt different, and now I could at least understand why I am the way I am. Most people can sense emotions, thoughts, and physical sensation from others, but an empath is someone who experiences them as their own. For me this can be incredibly stressful, draining, and confusing at times, so learning to manage my energy has really helped me.

There are many types of empaths and I am not going to go into detail on each one as that could be a book in itself. From the material I have studied I am what is called a Claircognizant empath as well as an Emotional one. A Claircognizant empath possesses a strong inner knowing about other people and things. I can usually know when something doesn't feel right and when someone is lying or hiding something. I also can "know" certain things without being told, which is different from a clairvoyant who see things in their minds eye. And although most empaths are Emotional Empaths, there can be a variety of ways that people cope with this. Some empaths have difficulty setting boundaries, and because of their deep feelings for others they can overextend themselves in trying to help others. On the other hand, other empaths like me will isolate and just shut people out as a way of dealing with it.

If you are an empath you have most likely experienced challenges in managing your energy. I still encounter difficulties myself, but I can tell you the practices in this book have helped me. I also began to change the way I was looking at it. A part of me use to feel it was a curse and I wondered, "Why can't I be like other people?" But I now see it as a gift, it has really served me over the years in avoiding people and experiences that were not for my highest good. Instead of resenting it, I now ask my Higher Power, "How can I use this gift to better serve others and myself?"

When you are an empath it's also particularly important to invest your time in activities that will assist you in developing more mental, emotional, and spiritual balance. The more centered and grounded you are, the easier it will be to maintain your energy during challenging situations. The first thing you want to work on is raising your vibration, so you aren't attracting these negative experiences and people. I found meditation to be a great tool and we will touch more on that in the chapter on Action. Secondly, you need to be emotionally available to only your higher self and your internal guidance. Empaths tend to react and respond to other peoples' energies because they are so extremely sensitive. That's why your relationship with yourself and your Higher Power needs to be your top priority. Everything else in your life is just a reflection of how strong that relationship is. The more you develop this, the less you will be thrown off by others behavior and be able to maintain your personal equanimity.

Lastly, begin to honor your uniqueness and your needs and don't feel like you must justify why you are the way you are. A major breakthrough for me was to stop trying to fit into a mold that just wasn't me and not needing to defend myself. For example, I have lived alone for over 25 years, and I love it. In fact, I can still remember the first day in my own apartment and how incredible it felt to have my own personal space. I felt truly joyful and peaceful. I also really enjoy traveling alone and have gone on numerous trips to all-inclusive resorts, cruises, and even to Italy for two weeks by myself. Most people cannot relate to this and tend to view it with skepticism or judgement, which sometimes would bother me. I would find myself trying to explain myself, which would only reinforce the feeling that there was something wrong with me. I have learned over the years to embrace my individuality doing what makes me happy and disregard how others may perceive it.

Entertainment

The area of entertainment is a good place to examine when you are wanting to transform your energy. In our society we tend to gravitate towards drama and excitement, in fact it can almost be a compulsion or addicting. The majority of your emotions are generated from what you are observing, so it's important to eval-uate if what you are focused on may be affecting your attraction point. I am not suggesting that you auto-matically eliminate all these activities, but if you find something is having a negative effect on you, then you might want to consider reducing the time you spend engaged in it. Or ask yourself, why you are attracted to this if it produces a negative feeling inside you?

The more you raise your energetic set point and maintain it, the more sensitive you will become to activities that may affect it. I noticed it first in music. I used to be drawn to all those heartbreak love songs and it was a major awakening when I realized I was just reinforcing that negative energy. I did not eliminate those old favorite love songs, but I did stop connecting all the old "drama" from the past to them. And now when I do listen to them, instead of recreating that old energy, I honor and appreciate my past and how far I have come over the years.

How would you rate the Movies and TV programs you frequently watch? How do they make you feel? I have a friend who loves watching survival programs and is always trying to get me to watch them. I have absolutely no desire to whatsoever, I would much rather focus my attention on people who are thriving, a romantic comedy, or even something educational. What type of energy do crime series or horror movies generate? It's all about how it makes you feel. Maybe it feels adventurous or suspenseful, only you can decide what's best for you and how it's affecting you. The news can also be very distressing, addictive and usually comes from a place of wanting to be informed. I personally feel it would be much more productive to put your energy towards creating a fabulous life, then focusing on terrible things that you have no control over. I believe watching the news right before you go to bed is probably one of the worst things you can do for your health. Very seldom do they focus on anything positive, and I see little value in it.

Once when I was in a spiritual book club I noticed that every book would start with all the pain and suffering the writer had gone through to get to where they were. I would usually skip those chapters because I was in an incredibly positive state, and I could feel the negative pull it was having on me. I eventually dropped out of the club because I was looking to be uplifted and empowered and I wasn't getting that from the books that were being selected. This is all very personal, so you really must observe how you feel and if it's something you want to change. Keep in mind, however, that most of us are offering our vibration to what we are observing, so limiting the amount of time in some of these activities can be very beneficial to your overall wellbeing.

In conclusion, you can't possibly control everything in your life. Other people, the political arena, the stock market, pollution, climate change, pandemics, other countries, different religions, and the list goes on. But you can change how you react emotionally. Pain is inevitable in our lives and a completely natural and sometimes necessary experience. Very often pain can be a catalyst for growth as well as stimulate desires and expansion. Suffering, however, is hanging on to the negative experience and not permitting yourself to move forward with the wisdom and insight you gained from the experience. When we worry about repeating the mistakes of the past, continue to tell our old negative stories, and live in fear trying to control people and circumstances we are actually remaining a vibrational match to the very thing we are trying to avoid. Over time as you practice these techniques you will see how great it feels to manage your emotional energy.

Chapter Highlights

- Our emotions are an indicator of where we are vibrating on various subjects and what the Law of Attraction is responding to.

- Our emotions can tell us whether we are lining up with the essence of our desire or lack of it.

- The emotional scale by Abraham Hicks is a great tool as it illustrates the progression from negative emotions to positive ones.

- Even our negative emotions serve a purpose. A constructive way to work through them is by using the Emotional Release Letter and the Soothe and Uplift letter.

- There are several challenges you may experience when trying to improve your emotions. One is feeling bad about having the negative emotions and another is trying to go from a very negative emotion to a very positive one too quickly.

- It's not necessary to always be in complete joy, and it's unrealistic to think you should be. The main goal is to ease any tension and then direct your focus in areas that you enjoy.

- Fine tuning is taking energy management to the next level and really paying close attention to precisely how you are feeling. These subtle energetic shifts can be extremely powerful.

- If you are an empath it's important to invest your time in activities that will assist you in developing more mental, emotional, and spiritual balance. The more centered and grounded you are the easier it will be to maintain your energy during challenging situations.

- The more you raise your energetic set point and maintain it the more sensitive you will become to activities that may affect it.

- Evaluating the type of entertainment you partake in can be very beneficial.

- Pain is inevitable in our lives and a completely natural and sometimes necessary experience. Suffering, however, is hanging on to the negative experience and not permitting yourself to move forward with the wisdom and insight you gained from the experience.

CHAPTER 6
Beliefs

There is one grand lie-that we are limited. The only limits we
have are the limits we believe. --Wayne Dyer

The next ingredient in the Magic Potion is your beliefs.
Our beliefs are habitual thought patterns that we no
longer question but accept as our truth. They have been
programmed into our subconscious over time and control
how we perceive and respond to our environment, as well
as what we attract into our lives. The beliefs you have
about yourself, other people, and life shape who you are
and who you will become. Many of our beliefs were
formed in childhood where we just accepted the
information that was given to us without any
discernment. They were imbedded in us by our family,
teachers or authority figures and are deeply engraved in
our thinking. So much of the time we are responding to
life and circumstances based on our beliefs without
questioning the validity of them.

The beliefs you have can be positive or limiting, and you are the only one who can decide how they are affecting your life. In this chapter, you will be working on becoming aware of your limiting beliefs and reframing them. This can be very challenging as sometimes they are stored in your subconscious mind, and you aren't really aware of them. It is not enough to just uncover these beliefs and thought patterns, you also need to replace them as well as the emotions tied to them. I hear so many people say how hard this is to do, and I agree that it does take a significant amount of effort to break these connections that have been wired for years. But I would have to say it is far more difficult to live your life controlled by limiting beliefs and destructive thought patterns. A powerful question to ask yourself is, "If I continue to hold on to this limiting belief what will my life look like ten years from now?" Then start to envision what your life could look like without this belief.

The sub-conscious mind makes up about 90 percent of the total mind and is where the majority of your beliefs are stored. I personally do not see great value in trying to go back and uncover all your negative beliefs and rehash all your childhood memories or traumas. There may be some benefit in this, but if a limiting belief or trauma has not yet been healed or resolved you will see it playing out in your present experiences in your relationships, finances, or possibly a health challenge. And, when it does surface in the present, the thoughts and emotions tied to it are more clear and vivid. You have a far better chance of healing and reframing now, as opposed to trying to recall something that happened many years ago. And you also have the benefit of viewing the belief from your newfound perspective, as opposed to when you may have felt helpless and victimized. It would be much more beneficial to direct your thoughts and emotions to creating the future you want, than stirring up old negative experiences. The present moment is all you ever need to heal. Only you can decide what's best for you but challenging your beliefs and questioning whether they are serving you or not is a great place to start.

The Four R'S

There are four steps to begin with in transforming your beliefs. I refer to them as the Four R's. They are: Realization, Refrain, Release, and Reframe.

Your beliefs are either inherited or formed from personal experience. Inherited beliefs are formed in our earlier years and taught to us either directly, or indirectly by just observing the behaviors of those close to us. A lot of these are in our sub-conscious, but we can be conscious of them as well. I was once having a discussion with a friend of mine on the subject of aging and assisted suicide and I expressed that in some instances I felt it was more humane to release someone from their suffering if it was a terminal illness. My friend's response was, "the way I was raised we don't believe that". Now, I am in no way challenging anyone's belief on this subject as it's very personal, and I totally respect that people see this differently. What I did find peculiar was how her response was "we" and she was almost 50 years old. She just accepted this as her truth without questioning it. Then about five years later the subject came up again and she was in favor of assisted suicide, so I asked why she had changed her viewpoint. She explained that after seeing what her mother went through in making her transition that she now has a totally different perspective. So now her belief is from personal experience as opposed to being inherited.

In looking at transforming your beliefs a great question to ask yourself is, "Is this belief serving me?" For my friend it apparently was not, as she held that belief for her entire life and then one experience completely changed her viewpoint. We may even want to question our beliefs formed from personal experience. For example, if someone had a partner that was unfaithful in a relationship, they may find it difficult to trust. Instead of starting each new relationship with confidence in the new partner, they start wondering if this person will be unfaithful too. Then because they have established that energetic setpoint they continue to attract the same situation over and over which then will become rooted as a belief. And they clearly have the evidence to prove it from their failed relationships, but this might be a belief worth questioning if it's creating pain and conflict for them.

Realization

The first step in transforming a belief is becoming aware of it. As I previously stated, I do not see a lot of value in going back into your past trying to uncover all your limiting beliefs, as this can really stir up a lot of negative emotions. Remember the Law of Attraction is always responding to your emotions and even the thought pattern of thinking you need to "fix" yourself can be a powerful attraction point, implying there is currently something wrong with you. That is why I recommend just letting your current experiences naturally reveal to you the beliefs you may want to reframe. There are so many beliefs stored in the subconscious on so many different topics, but the ones that are most relevant are the ones you will see playing out in your life and creating distress and limitations in the present.

If you have an experience or area of your life that is troubling you, you can start by asking yourself what kind of belief or beliefs would create this? If you have been struggling with something for a while there's a good chance there are some limiting beliefs associated with it. Writing the ERL (Emotional Release Letter) is a great tool for uncovering underlying beliefs. When you go back and read what you wrote it can be very helpful in discovering what might be a contributing factor. Or I will request in an affirmation or my SUL (Soothe and Uplift Letter) that, "any limiting beliefs or thought patterns that may be bringing about this unwanted experience be revealed to me at the perfect time." And then I just do my best to let go knowing it's all unfolding perfectly.

Refrain

The next step in transforming your beliefs is Refrain. What this means is that once you have discovered an unwanted belief you want to give as little attention to it as possible, both mentally and verbally. A great place to start is not to talk about or affirm the belief you are wanting to change. I always hear people say, "I can't afford that." I stopped using that phrase as a teenager and it has served me very well. I reframed it by saying "I have other areas I choose to spend my money at this time." This was just a first baby step but at least I began taking my power back. Or just don't say anything. It is crucial not to engage in your "negative stories" or participate in negative conversations if you are wanting to change that area in your life. This can be problematic at times as others tend to want to talk about all the bad things going on and their challenges. The less you join in on these conversations the less others will look to involve you, and the more you raise your vibration and stop attracting these types of individuals into your life.

Negative thoughts can take more discipline to refrain from because we are constantly thinking, and it seems our minds never shut up. Thoughts come and go but what determines their attraction power is how much "airtime" you give them, and the emotions attached to them. Changing your focus is a very effective tool to use when you are experiencing undesirable thoughts. You can state an affirmation or invoke one of your images to start breaking the pattern of these thoughts and beliefs. One thing you want to take notice of is if you are rejecting these thoughts or beliefs and getting frustrated with yourself for experiencing them. Some of these beliefs are deeply seated and have been programmed in you for years and years, so they don't typically disappear overnight. Your goal is to transform them and not reject them because your dissatisfaction with these limiting beliefs will just reinforce the very thing you want to free yourself from. Allow yourself to "feel" the emotions that are connected to these beliefs even if they are negative, and then give thanks that they are guiding you when you are off track. The more you can be at peace with what you are feeling, the easier it will be to release these old thought patterns and create a new vision for yourself and your life.

Release

Another step to transforming beliefs is through what I call the Release step. Once you become aware of a belief that you do not feel is in your best interest, you can start the process of transforming the energy around it. You may want to start with an ERL to see what your attachment is to this belief. It may have to do with caring how others think or will feel, this typically occurs if we are challenging a childhood belief that was instilled by loved ones. Or maybe you are trying too hard, comparing yourself to others or where you think you should be. When you use the ERL and are completely honest about how you are feeling and not holding back, you can usually gain a lot of insight into areas where you might feel stuck or are having difficulty letting go.

It's important to understand that a lot of the beliefs you have were usually developed for good reasons at that time. For example, if you were in an abusive relationship you may have developed beliefs to protect yourself in the future from being hurt, but that belief is now inhibiting you from opening up and trusting others. If on some level you feel this belief is serving you it may be very difficult to just release it. It can sometimes help to start with looking at the negative emotion attached to the belief and try to separate the emotion from the experience. In the example I gave about the abusive relationship, several emotions could be tied to the inability to trust such as fear, suspicion, feeling guarded, or withdrawn. Once you have uncovered the emotions, you can now utilize some of the processes to start realigning your energy. I personally find images to be a very effective tool to ease tension related to negative energy. You want to find images that embody the way you would feel if you were free from these unwanted emotions, then when these feelings surface you can immediately conjure up the image and begin to dissipate the negative energy.

Reframe

The final step in transforming your beliefs is to reframe them. Once you ease your attachment and some of the negative energy connected to the belief it's time to re-direct your energy to the greater vision you have for yourself and your life. Ask yourself what your life would look like without this limiting belief? How would you feel? What possibilities would be open to you? What choices would you make? Who would be there and what type of people would you choose to surround yourself with? What new belief would you need to instill to be in alignment with what you are wanting? I would recommend writing it out and just like with affirmations keeping it in the present tense as well as reading it out loud on occasion. When you are reading your Reframe Statement (RS) pay attention to how you are feeling as this will guide you as to how close you are to lining up with it.

If I feel it's a big stretch for me to line my energy up with my (RS), I may write a transitional one to assist me in getting closer. You really want to play with this and let your emotions be your guide. If you are reading your RS and it's bringing up feelings of frustration, impatience, or anxiety then you need to ease that tension. This may seem tedious at times, but if you are looking to transform beliefs that have been embedded in your subconscious mind for your entire life, it may take some time. The important thing is to just do your best to have fun with this and know you are in your perfect place and it's all unfolding as it should. Even the slightest shifts of energy can bring considerable results, starting with how much better you will feel. It's just like learning any new skill. In the beginning it can seem awkward and challenging but the more you do it the better you will be at it, so give yourself a chance to utilize these exercises and see the improvement in your life.

Examples

Here are some examples of Reframing Statements I wrote on weight loss. It's extremely important that you feel positive and uplifted when you read your RS. If you are feeling doubtful, frustrated, or impatient you may need to ease into your vision. If it's an area you have been struggling with for a while you may want to start out being somewhat vague and then get more detailed as you progress.

Example One

I am ready to transform my energy in this area of my life. I am open and receptive to the guidance from my higher self and the Universe to reveal to me what I need to know and how to do it. I trust in myself and my Higher Power to support me through this transformation. I'm excited. I have faith in this process and in my ability to transform my energy. I now choose to line my energy up with the greater part of me and allow it to express through me looking absolutely fabulous at my ideal weight, feeling good about myself and making choices my body responds well to.

Example Two

It feels so good to be improving my energy around this subject of my weight and my physical appearance. It's so awesome to see my body responding so well and I feel inspired to act in ways that support my desire. I am really changing at my core and I'm very happy with the progress I am making. It feels so good to just release the struggle and be at peace with where I am. I take note of my successes and allow myself to feel proud of my accomplishments. I feel like a new person connected to my higher self and my Higher Power.

Example Three

I now see myself at my ideal weight feeling a total sense of presence in my body. I feel lean, strong, and bubbling with energy and vitality. All my clothes look fabulous on me and fit just perfectly. It feels great to be at my perfect weight and maintain it.

It's so nice having a loving and appreciative relationship with food. It feels good to have so much variety and be flexible and spontaneous. I'm enjoying the foods I eat as well as the portions and feel satisfied and comfortable. Planning my meals is fun and I'm finding so many recipes that are easy to prepare, taste fabulous and my body responds well to.

I wake up every day inspired to make choices that support me in living at my highest potential. I replace old, practiced thought patterns and vibrations with a new vision of myself. I love, honor, and appreciate my body and it's responding fabulously to my new energetic setpoint.

Can you feel the slight progression of energy in these

three examples? This is what transforming energy looks like. You have to feel your way through it tweaking it as you go. Clarity is awesome when you are in a positive state as it can really build great momentum, but if you find it unsettling then you might want to be less specific. In the first two examples I mostly concentrated on transforming my energy as opposed to all the details, which is a great starting point. You may choose to write something entirely different. Remember, the Law is not responding to your words, it responds to how you feel so anyway you can get yourself to feel better about what you are wanting is the ultimate goal.

As you start developing your own practice you will really start to get in touch with your attraction point. You will also probably discover that it varies in different areas of your life. For instance, you may have great relationships and friendships but struggle with your finances or have health challenges. Take a look at the areas in your life where you feel successful and observe what your habitual thoughts are on that subject and how you feel about it and talk about it. Then compare it to an area that you may be struggling with or feel you are lacking. I'm sure you will see that the subjects you think and feel more positive about tend to be going better for you and you will see a definite correlation with your beliefs and what you are currently experiencing. As you reframe your beliefs you will begin to change your attraction point as well as build your confidence so that your actions reflect this. You see possibility and opportunity where before you may have felt stuck. It opens the door to many options you may not have felt were possible to you and now you have the courage and confidence to walk through them.

Health

In Chapter Three, we briefly touched on the biology of your beliefs as well as epigenetics and how our environment and our perception of it can greatly influence how a gene expresses. Our beliefs about health greatly influence our physical wellbeing, and most will agree if we don't have good health if affects all areas of our lives. Yet so many people in our society are experiencing all kinds of health challenges and are unaware of how much influence they have in the quality of their life. Eating healthy, getting proper rest and exercise, as well as reducing stress to improve your health is pretty common knowledge, but the majority of individuals never question how their thought patterns can contribute to disease as well as recovering from an illness or injury.

For example, feel the difference between the terms "Battling Illness" and "Creating Health." How you feel about what you are doing has a major impact on how your body responds. Acting from a place of fear or combatting something is far different than acting from a place of feeling empowered. Even the major focus on prevention can have an underlying vibration that you are trying to stop something bad from happening to you. That's not to say that you want to ignore taking preventative measures, but it is being aware of how you feel about it and if there is any negative energy associated to the matter. Once you are able to free up this negative energy you are opening up for the natural life force to flow more fully through you, to rejuvenate and restore you.

It's a major misconception that doctors can heal you, it is always your body's own innate intelligence that heals and restores. Think about when you have a wound and have to get stitches. The doctor may stitch you up and prescribe an antibiotic to prevent infection, but it is the body that mends itself back together again. The drug that was prescribed is battling an infection, but it is not restoring the body. Doctors can provide an environment for a healing to take place, but it is your body's intelligence that will ultimately heal you. I am in no way trying to undermine the marvelous work provided by the health care industry and all the good they provide, but I do want you to understand the miracle and divine intelligence of the body you were born with. Too often we rely on doctors to "fix" us as opposed to making the choices and taking the actions that will assist your body in staying well. Believing in the Divine Intelligence flowing through every cell in your body will greatly enhance your overall health and wellbeing.

Thinking you can take a pill that is going to resolve a health challenge is another misconception. It's very misfortunate how often a drug is prescribed, as opposed to seeing if there is any action or lifestyle change we could make that could work as well. The problem is people want a quick remedy and they don't want to put the effort into other options that may be available. And the sad thing about it is the pill is usually not correcting the ailment, but only camouflaging the symptoms. You may be finding relief from the drug but why are you experiencing the symptoms to begin with? Your body is trying to communicate with you and instead of listening you are just taking a pill that may not be correcting what is wrong and can be causing serious side effects. I want to make it very clear that I am not suggesting that you should stop taking any of your medication or not follow your doctor's instructions. I do feel, however, that it's very important to look at your beliefs about how much power you have in your healing and try to develop a stronger relationship with your body. If you combine that with a health care provider you have confidence in you will have a lot of influence in your overall health.

Several years ago I was experiencing pain in my chest area and when I went to see my primary doctor he said he thought it was my gall bladder. The symptoms weren't terrible, so I decided to do a series of cleanses that seemed to help. He did offer me a prescription and wanted to do an ultrasound, but I always prefer to try natural remedies first whenever possible. Over time the pain kept coming back so I decided to go see a specialist. I personally am not a fan of seeing doctors, but I felt this was going on long enough that it would be a good idea to talk to an expert. Prior to my appointment I did my energy work to relieve my tension about seeing a doctor, as well as asking for divine guidance and being open and receptive to any insight as to why I was experiencing the discomfort.

The doctor first asked me a series of questions and

listened but didn't really offer any feedback. He then proceeded to schedule a colonoscopy and an endoscopy to take a closer look at things. Right before I was leaving his office something inside nudged me to inquire deeper into a question he had asked. He wanted to know if I ate before I went to bed at night and I told him I didn't have a typical nine to five job so I would eat dinner late on occasions. When I inquired as to why he asked me that question he said that lying down after you eat can sometimes cause problems. He said he'd know more once we have the tests results. Once I got home I immediately Googled lying down after eating and discovered that this can cause the acids used in digesting the food to irritate the esophagus. What I then realized was after dinner I would lie on the couch and watch TV, especially in the winter months and that is when my symptoms would get worse. I immediately canceled all the tests and told him I wanted to see if adjusting this behavior would alleviate my symptoms, and sure enough it did.

What really baffles me to this day is that if I would not have taken the initiative to ask the doctor that question, I would have just continued with this behavior without ever realizing what was going on. I would have taken all the tests and he probably would have prescribed me drugs or some procedure and all I needed to do was sit up straight for an hour after I ate. I understand the doctor was just doing his job and had he not prescribed those tests he could be liable, but I cannot understand why he didn't at least advise me not to lie down after eating. That is why it is so important to listen to your body and your own inner guidance as well as the doctors. I did benefit from going to an expert but ultimately took the action that I felt was best for me, as well as trusting my body's own ability to heal itself.

Having a loving relationship with food is one of the most important things you can do in creating health, yet so many of us are constantly struggling with this. These days it seems anything you eat is bad for you in some way, so it can feel very confusing to know who and what to listen to. And if we are eating food while feeling all this confusion, anxiety, and doubt we are definitely affecting how we are metabolizing our food. Think about the various foods that affect people so differently. One person can eat all they want and never gain a pound, while another seems to struggle with their weight no matter how careful they are. We generally say "it's my metabolism" not realizing that our thoughts and feelings about the foods are influencing the way our body responds. You can't eat something that you feel might be bad for you and be in harmony with it.

I suggest you make friends with food and follow your own inner guidance as opposed to navigating through all the conflicting information out there. If you are uncertain then ask the Universe and your body for direction, and then be open and receptive to what comes up. This is how you will develop a healthy connection with food as well as your own inner being. Take time to bless your food before you eat it feeling love and appreciation for it, expecting it to nourish and restore you. You will be amazed at how this action alone can really affect your overall wellbeing. Food is what sustains us so cleaning up any unwanted beliefs in this area is a great way to positively affect every area of our life.

When it comes to our health there are so many different paths to choose from; Western Medicine, Eastern Medicine, Holistic, Alternative, Ayurvedic, Functional and the list goes on. There is so much evidence that different people respond differently to the same treatments and medications, which is why individual beliefs need to be factored into the equation. How much confidence you have in your doctor and what he is prescribing, as well as your beliefs about aging, dying and your body's own ability to restore and heal itself are going to have a major impact on how your body responds. Creating health is taking an active role in your health and wellbeing. Once you start discovering beliefs that you want to transform you can begin the process of reframing them as well as directing your thoughts and emotions towards more positive outcomes.

Money

Money is a subject that can trigger a lot of beliefs, and how you feel about money can have a huge influence on your quality of life. Money is tied to our very survival as it is a means of exchange for goods and services. You cannot live comfortably in this physical universe without food, shelter, and clothing at a minimum, and yet so many people are very conflicted when it comes to their desire for more. Feel energetically the difference in "surviving" and "thriving." Obviously thriving feels much more freeing, yet most of us are programmed to believe that there is not enough, or that we are greedy if we desire or have too much. Both of these thought patterns come from a belief in scarcity and clearing that belief is essential if you are to create a life that allows you to express your highest potential. There is nothing virtuous about living in poverty, struggling to make ends meet, or feeling guilty when you are experiencing abundance and wealth. In fact to the contrary the more affluent you are, the more you have to share and circulate, as well as support your personal and spiritual growth.

I was raised by a single mom with three children in the 60's and have worked my entire life on clearing this belief in scarcity. I remember when I was a young child at the grocery store with my mom and seeing her put meat in her purse for our dinner, and she felt no guilt whatsoever. In fact I think she felt that it was her duty to provide for her children and she was going to do it however she could. Seeing this behavior growing up influenced me to shoplift when I was a teenager, and I too felt very little remorse. I knew it was wrong, but just saw it as a way to get the things I wanted that I could not afford. It wasn't until I started learning about how our beliefs can affect our experiences that I changed my perception. I realized that stealing was not only reinforcing a belief in scarcity, but also a belief that I wasn't capable or worthy of earning enough income to provide for my needs and desires. I stopped that behavior when I was fifteen, which was the first step in changing those beliefs. Another area people can struggle with is feeling guilty or uncomfortable about their personal financial successes and wealth. This also comes from a belief in scarcity, except now this belief is projected at others and their ability to provide for themselves. It may feel like it's denying reality when you think of all the poverty and injustice in the world, but when we view others as helpless we are only reinforcing the very energy that is keeping them stuck in their current situation. The greatest gift we have to offer others is a belief in them and their personal power and feeling apologetic for your achievements or wealth is not serving them. Your success is a beacon for them to aspire to and has the potential to inspire them to their own greatness. When you inspire someone you are stimulating them to desire and want more, which is where all creation begins.

Now you may feel motivated to assist those less fortunate than you, which is a wonderful thing. Giving to those who are in need can be very beneficial to both parties and is certainly a very honorable and generous act. What is most important is the energy behind the giving. When it's from a place of joy and being able to share your blessings with others, it can be a very rewarding experience. If you are giving because you feel obligated or feeling sorry for those you are giving to, then you might want to find a way of reframing that. Whether you decide to give or not is irrelevant, what's really important is to evaluate the energy behind the giving. When you give because you feel guilty about your own wealth, or you feel that these individuals are unable to care for themselves you are depleting everyone's energy. Seeing others as incomplete or inadequate is not serving them and robbing them energetically. What others really want more than what you are giving them, is to know they can achieve it themselves. I love the quote "Give a man a fish, feed him for a day, teach a man to fish, feed him for a lifetime." The greatest gift you can offer them is seeing them as a powerful creator, regardless of the current situation they may be living.

Circulation is another form of giving that is very often overlooked. Some will argue that because you are getting something in return it's not really giving, but I feel that is a misconception. Think about before money and currency existed and when the exchange of goods and services was all there was. Each party was giving value and feeling valued which created a sense of unity with their fellow man. The only difference today is that money is a symbol of goods and services, and when you are spending it you are circulating your good which is benefiting others. Life is a constant recycling of energy, we breathe in we breathe out. Both acts support our wellbeing and a heathy balance between these two acts is very productive.

How do you feel when you are spending your money? Do you feel depleted, like there's never enough and a constant struggle to make ends meet? Do you feel remorseful when you make frivolous purchases, feeling like you should be giving more to charity? When others have more than you are you resentful or jealous? Do you feel they have more than their share and they should be more generous? These questions are not about right and wrong or passing judgement, but how you feel about these subjects can be a wonderful guide to see where you are energetically. Circulating your wealth is a marvelous way to promote joy and prosperity in the lives of others and acknowledging that will raise your vibration on this subject. If you are feeling insecure with your supply or offended by others affluence, then you may have some beliefs in scarcity or your own personal worth that you might want to evaluate. The Universe is abundant, plentiful, and infinite by nature and the more you can line your energy up with that concept, the more you will attract more prosperity into your experience.

It has been said that the love of money is the root of all evil. Money is merely a piece of paper used as a medium to exchange goods and services, and there's nothing wrong with feeling love and appreciation for it. If man chooses to use it for corruption or exploitation that is coming from a place of fear not love. In fact I personally believe that fear is the root of all evil. If you look at why people do harmful things to others, I think you will find some level of fear underlying it. Fear is being separated from who you really are and your Higher Power, which is why it feels so awful. When people are in a state of fear they are disconnected from their higher being and desperately trying to get their power back. It may be the way they are perceiving the situation, but to them the feeling of vulnerability and helplessness is very real.

These are just a few examples of some very common beliefs that may be interfering with your financial success. Once you start clearing them it's like the layers of an onion and you will continue to uncover more and more. Money is a fun place to start with using some of the exercises offered in this book, as it's easy to measure your results. There is nothing more rewarding than being able to provide for yourself, your loved ones and feel independent and self-sufficient. When we break out of survival mode we can begin to flourish in all areas of our life, tending to our spiritual needs and expressing ourselves creatively. We are in a great place to serve others and share and circulate our good with love and appreciation.

Relationships

Relationships can be very rewarding and yet very challenging at the same time. Our beliefs can strongly influence how we interact with others and the type of relationships we attract. The most common misconception about relationships that creates the most conflict is expecting others to provide a feeling of connection that can only be achieved through our personal connection with the Divine Energy flowing through all creation. When we look to others to act in certain ways so that we can experience more joy we may temporarily feel good, but as soon as their behavior changes we revert right back to where we were. We then blame them for how we are feeling, when it is really our disconnection from the energy of love that was flowing through us when we focused on them, that is creating the negative feeling. Our relationships are an avenue for us to experience great joy and satisfaction, but it's important to realize that when things go awry, it's not the person that is causing your internal conflict. It is you losing your connection with the Divine Energy flowing through you that is creating the discord you are feeling. When you are in alignment with the Source of all Love and Life, you do not need others to behave in a certain way for you to be happy. This does not mean that you will allow others to treat you badly, you just won't be dependent on them for your joy.

We are also programed by our families and society on what acceptable relationships look like. Take marriage for example, it's impossible not to be influenced by our cultural beliefs about it. I'm not saying that's a bad thing, I just feel it's important to be able to distinguish this programming and decide if it's something that is for your highest good. I have never been married, and I am very happy with my life and how it has unfolded. I had always assumed I would get married and was engaged once in my mid-twenties. At the time a lot of my friends were getting married and I thought it was just what everyone did. I don't think I ever questioned if it was the right thing for me, and just went along with the "norm". I remember feeling so uncomfortable in my thirties when relatives or other people would question me as to why I was not married yet, and I would feel I had to explain myself, which was not a great use of my energy. So I came up with the response "I guess I never thought of marriage as the only option in life." It was great because it really took the pressure off me to explain why I wasn't married, and it gave them an opportunity to look at their own belief systems. Let me be clear that I am not condemning marriage in any way, and I have many friends and relatives who have wonderful marriages. I just think it's important to evaluate some of these common beliefs as opposed to just going along with the "norm" like I almost did.

Another area people tend to struggle with in relationships is feeling responsible for others' happiness and wellbeing. It can be very difficult to watch those we love suffering and wanting to relieve that and be there for them is totally understandable as well as admirable. You just have to realize that you must manage your own emotions first. When you come from a place of your own balanced energy you have the most to give. This has always been especially difficult for me when I feel those I love are not making the choices that would be for their highest good and I would truly fear for their welfare. One technique I found very beneficial is just focusing on how much I love this person, as you cannot hold the energy of fear and love at the same time. This is a great way to shift your energy in the moment and stop the negative emotions from escalating. Then when I have more time I will Reframe how I am seeing them and their circumstances and line my energy up with a greater vision of them. Some may feel this is being insensitive or not being compassionate to the pain they are dealing with, but you connecting to their negative experience is not assisting them either. Connecting with your love for them and a greater vision you have for them is truly one of the most beneficial things you can do.

Or how about when others feel we should be different to please them. This is another common conflict we experience in relationships when we feel we are responsible for another's experience. Now if pleasing this

EVERYDAY MAGIC

person brings you joy, then by all means follow your bliss. But if you are feeling resentful or if it's interfering with your own needs, then you may want to evaluate what is best for you in the situation. This may sound selfish and go against what you were taught about being kind and thoughtful, but if you are jeopardizing your own happiness then you aren't really serving others. In fact, trying to act in ways to meet others' demands is not allowing them to take responsibility for their own energy management. You are making them rely on you for their emotional stability as opposed to learning the skills necessary to relieve their own personal discomfort. All relationships will benefit when we stop expecting others to do for us what only we can do for ourselves.

Relationships, money, and health have various beliefs associated with them. The important thing is to start evaluating your own beliefs and decide for yourself if they are empowering you or disempowering you. If you are struggling in any of these areas it might be helpful to question if there could be a limiting or false belief connected, and if it's how you really feel, or whether you are just responding from your conditioning. You cannot create beyond your current beliefs. If you believe in limitations, you will not see the possibilities or opportunities available to you. Your belief will continue to attract the same old experiences until you redirect that energy and establish a new attraction point. In conclusion, just know that there is a constant stream of well-being, abundance, and love. You don't have to make anything happen, you are just removing the blocks that are interfering with the flow of vibrant health, unlimited abundance, and loving relationships from pouring into your experience. By letting go of your limiting beliefs and reframing how you see yourself, your loved ones, and your life, you are becoming a magnet for wonderful things to begin to manifest into your experience.

Chapter Highlights

- Our beliefs are habitual thought patterns that we no longer question but accept as our truth. They have been programmed in our subconscious over time and control how we perceive and respond to our environment, as well as what we attract into our lives.

- It is not enough to just uncover restricting beliefs and thought patterns, we also need to replace them as well as the emotions tied to them.

- It is not necessary to go back and uncover all your negative beliefs and rehash all your childhood traumas. If a belief pattern is a strong point of attraction you will see it manifesting in your present experience.

- There are four steps to begin with in transforming your beliefs that I refer to as the Four R's. Realization-Refrain-Release-Reframe.

- Once you ease your attachment and some of the negative energy connected to the belief it's time to re-direct your energy to the greater vision you have for yourself and your life.

- Our beliefs about health greatly influence our physical wellbeing, and most will agree if we don't have good health if affects all areas of our lives.

- Money is a subject that can trigger a lot of beliefs, and how you feel about money can have a huge influence on your quality of life.

- The most common misconception about relationships is expecting others to provide a feeling of connection that can only be achieved through our own personal connection with the Divine Energy flowing through all creation.

- There is a constant stream of well-being, abundance, and love. You don't have to make anything happen, you are just removing the blocks that are interfering with the flow of vibrant health, unlimited abundance, and loving relationships from pouring into your experience.

CHAPTER 7

Action

There is not enough action in the world to make up for misaligned energy. --Abraham-Esther Hicks

When I first heard the above statement it really resonated with me. I had always been extremely action orientated, constantly setting goals, pushing myself, and actually feeling guilty if I was not working hard or even taking time to relax. In fact, our entire society is very action orientated and really values hard work and being productive, so we are all somewhat programed to the idea that hard work equals results and success. Now there is nothing wrong with being motivated and putting effort and time into the activities and matters that are important to you, but it's extremely valuable to do so from a place of alignment and enthusiasm. When you make it a priority to manage your personal energy first and foremost, your life will become more effortless, and you will start attracting people and circumstances that are in alignment with your desires and intentions. Feel the difference between being driven and being inspired. Energetically, being driven feels like pushing yourself and being more forceful, whereas inspired feels more like being drawn to something and there's an easiness about it. As we discussed in the previous chapter, these subtle differences in our energy can have a huge impact on what we attract into our lives, as well as the quality of our lives and the joy we experience during the process.

You may be thinking, what about undesirable circumstances and responsibilities? How can I possibly align my energy with these areas that I feel are my duty or are currently in my surroundings when inside I feel totally opposed to them. Well the first step is to make peace with where you are. You can't get from point A to point Z starting from point D, you can only start from where you are and being unhappy with where you are is only reinforcing the very circumstance you are wanting to be free of. Making peace with what is does not mean that you are accepting an intolerable situation, it's standing in your present circumstances knowing that you are one with an All-Powerful, All-Knowing, Infinite Being. You may not be able to immediately change something in your experience, but you certainly have the power to change your emotions and energy about it.

Decision

Making a decision is a great place to start your action

journey. Once you make a decision and line your energy and action up with it, the Law of Attraction has a clear signal to respond to. When you are not sure about what to do, searching for answers, or struggling with perfectionism it can lead to procrastination. This weakens your attraction point. It's usually more productive to make a decision, you can always adjust as you go. Stepping in the wrong direction can sometimes be more beneficial than doing nothing at all, at least you will learn and gain more information and insight. To stay in a place of confusion, not take action or be unhappy in your current circumstances is still a decision, even if you are not consciously making it.

Sometimes it's helpful prior to making a decision to contemplate how it will make you feel. For example, a friend of mine has a grandchild that he loves dearly and has practically raised him. The child's parents are very irresponsible so he has some conflicted energy about how much he should be assisting with raising their child. He feels very resentful, but at the same time very concerned for his grandchild's wellbeing. For him it would be far more difficult to abandon his grandson, than continue to enable the parents. For his own personal wellbeing it would be best to just make peace with his decision to assist with raising the child and put as much positive energy into that as possible. Feeling resentful or frustrated with the parents is a poor use of energy. If he is going to continue to assist, he might as well find a way to release those feelings and replace them with more positive ones. Another person in the same situation may have to set boundaries and let go if that would make them feel better. There is no right or wrong decision. But once that decision is made it's best to line your energy up with that decision.

When you make a decision it's important that your actions are in accord with that decision as well. You want your behavior to be in agreement with your decision and something you feel good about. Say for example you decide you want to lose weight, yet you continue to eat unhealthy foods that you know will prevent you from doing this. If you do something that you think is bad for you then you are not going to have good results. That's why it's important to energetically line up with your decision and actions. When you get your energy aligned you start to build momentum and it starts to feel effortless because they are now working together. It's like a car going downhill and you no longer need to push the gas petal.

Split Energy

Split Energy is very common but can sometimes be very difficult to reveal. Remember the example that I gave under conflicting desires of wanting to be in a relationship but at the same time really desiring a lot of personal space. When you have two conflicting desires that are both very important to you, you will probably see it reflecting in your manifestations. For the previous ex-ample I gave, it would be not to attract any relationships at all, attract someone who is emotionally unavailable or possibly attract short term relationships so that they will not interfere with need for personal space. If your manifestations are off because of split energy it can be helpful to ask yourself why you want these things and how you feel the one desire will jeopardize the other? This will help to guide you in clearing up the conflicting energy and then lining up with your desires in both areas.

Another type of split energy is you and your desire are a match, but what you think you want is not a match to your desire. When I was looking to buy a home there was a ranch house that I really wanted that was only on the market for one weekend and sold. This was during a time when the inventory for homes was very low and if there were any good homes out there they got swept up very quickly. So, I put in an offer with about five other buyers and it was not accepted. I was so disappointed and starting to get discouraged because I had been looking for a home for a long time. Looking back at that experience I can totally see that that house was not a match to my true desire. First of all, I don't even like ranch homes, what I really wanted was a cape cod. I much prefer having an upstairs and I wanted a home with a kitchen open to the living room, which was not possible in this home even if I removed a wall. So, when something you think you want doesn't manifest, do your best to know that the Universe is unlimited and all-knowing and that nothing can come between you and your good. That ranch home is about 10 blocks away from the cape cod that I currently live in. Occasionally I drive by it and give thanks that the Universal Intelligence new better than I did.

A very common conflict some people experience is that they lower their desire because they don't think what they want is possible. They look at their lives and their past and they become a vibrational match to that as opposed to what they really want. We have all heard the old saying "Don't get your hopes up too high" The main problem with this is that you can't undo a desire once it's been born, and you will always have a yearning. You can try and talk yourself out of it, but that is what is causing the split energy. This may be a time to look at your beliefs to see if there is something that is interfering. Or it may be that you are just used to your attraction point because it's comfortable and you may need to do some tweaking to raise your vibration to line up with what you truly desire.

Surrender

When you are clear on what you want, and you are doing your best to maintain a positive energy then surrendering the situation over to your Higher Power can be worthwhile. Sometimes people will be reluctant to surrender because they feel they are giving up or giving in which is not the case. When you surrender you are not giving up your desires, but you are releasing the struggle of trying to control the outcome. It can sometimes be challenging when you have a clear vision of what you want and yet you need to detach from the outcome. Even though we have ideas about how we want our good to manifest we also have access to an All-Knowing and All-

Powerful Being. When you have faith in the process and trust in your Higher Power you are opening yourself to all of the infinite possibilities available to you. When you surrender, you release the need for a physical manifestation and allow your energetic shift to be sufficient enough to feel complete in the moment.

Surrendering is not just "going with the flow" although that can be a component of it. Going with the flow can feel less resistant than trying to control outcomes and can sometimes be beneficial. However if you don't have a clear vision of what you want and an idea of the direction you would like your life to take, you can be like a feather in the wind. You may be more vulnerable to outside negative forces, or other peoples' agendas that may not be in line with what you really want. If going with the flow is bringing you joy, fulfillment and a sense of free-flowing energy that is a sign that you are on the right track. But if it feels like you are constantly compromising your will, or attracting experiences that are less than desirable, you may want to spend more time defining what you want and why you want it. This will assist in creating the essence of the desire as described in the previous chapter. Surrendering is still being very committed to your desires but releasing the need to control all the circumstances surrounding it. You adapt as you go and remain open to any guidance that is there to assist you on your journey.

When I think of surrender the serenity prayer always comes to mind. "God grant me the serenity to accept the things I cannot change, courage to change the things I can, and the wisdom to know the difference." This is especially relevant in relationships as we cannot control other people. When I was seventeen years old my mother took me to a therapist and wanted to put me in drug rehab. She saw the path I was on and was very concerned for my life and had no idea how to help me. During the session, I remember telling them that putting me in rehab would be a total waste, I had no intention to quit doing drugs and would just start right back up when I was released. To my surprise the therapist agreed with me. She then recommended that my mother continue the sessions, but she no longer wanted to see me as it would not be long until I was eighteen and would be of legal age. Looking back I realize how difficult that must have been for my mother to just let go of me and not try and control me or my destructive behaviors. But she did. She focused on working through her own personal matters, caring for her own needs, and no longer chose to involve herself with my problems. This may seem uncaring, but it was truly the best thing my mother could have done to help me. I didn't immediately quit doing drugs, but I was able to observe the transformation in my mom and learned how to take care of myself from her example. I eventually quit doing all drugs and put myself through college. Had my mother forced me into rehab, I may have rebelled, and things could have turned out very different.

Forgiveness

Right now you might be thinking "What does forgiveness have to do with action?" When you understand that there is a stream of wellbeing flowing through all creation, your job is to become an open channel for this good to flow through. With this in mind, a lot of your action may be about releasing lower energies that may be interfering with this flow in your life. Resentment and other negative emotions corrode the vessel that contains them, and that vessel is you. It's a common misconception that when you forgive you are doing it to release the individual who you feel has harmed you, but really the person you are freeing is yourself. Yet even when we have an intellectual understanding of this, it can be an extremely difficult thing to do when someone or something has caused us to experience great pain or disruption in our lives.

I personally struggled with understanding how to forgive for a long time. I truly wanted to forgive, and I knew it was harming me so much more than the person or experiences, I just didn't know how to do it. We hear all the time how important it is to forgive, but there is no set of instructions on how this is done. The first step is to be willing to forgive, because if you aren't willing then there is no going forward. Regardless of what happened the negative energy now resides in you, so it can help to separate the energy from the experience or person who caused it. When you do this it can make it much easier to be willing to forgive. Some of the negative energies associated with the inability to forgive are blame, anger resentment, feeling victimized, as well as guilt or remorse if you are the person you need to forgive. When you decide to take ownership of these feelings and believe in your ability to transform this energy, you are opening the doorway for the healing process to begin. Keep in mind it is a process and give yourself the time and space to work through your distress as pressuring yourself will only inflame the discomfort.

Once you are willing to forgive and accept responsibility for the negative emotions you are taking your power back. Feelings of blame and victimization are weakening your connection to your spirit, which is the very thing you need to assist you in your healing. Asking your Higher Power for guidance, insight and strength will begin to open your heart to healing. Life can be like a classroom and sometimes there's a lesson we need to learn, or we are being prepared for something in the future that we aren't even aware of. When you are able to separate the emotions from the harmful event or individual, and just view them as blocks of energy, you start to break the internal connections. This is extremely helpful in the process. You can also look to see if these particular emotions are reoccurring for you. If so you now have an opportunity to transform this energy, as opposed to reinforcing it. When you continue to hang on to any negative experience you become a vibrational match to the very thing that caused you harm to begin with.

Meditation

Meditation is a wonderful practice and another form of action that can assist you in releasing lower energy blocks. I studied Primordial Sound Meditation under Deepak Chopra in 1993 which used a mantra to help you quiet your mind. Today there are so many techniques available so you can explore your options and see what works for you. One common misconception about meditation is that you go into a trance for the entire time you are meditating and completely stop all thought. Because of this confusion some individuals will get frustrated when they are unable to achieve these altered states and give up. With practice you can certainly increase the time that you are able to stop your thoughts, but initially it's usually for very short time, especially if your mind is very active. I find meditating in the morning is better for me, before I start engaging in emails and other types of stimulating activities. It's a great way to ground and center yourself before starting your day.

One of the greatest benefits from developing a regular meditation practice is that you can give yourself some space from your thoughts and emotions, and you learn to gain more control over them. The majority of people are so engaged with their thoughts and emotions that they start to think that they are their thoughts and emotions. They don't realize that there is a part of them that is thinking the thoughts and feeling the emotions. I have heard it called the silent observer or witness, I like to call it our spirit. There is that presence within all of us that is experiencing the events in our lives as well as the corresponding thoughts and emotions. When we meditate we learn to quiet the constant dialogue we have going on in our head and just be. This happens when your thoughts subside, or you distance yourself from them by just observing them in a detached manner. During your meditation you will typically go in and out of these states and that's just fine. It's through this process that you will begin to not only realize, but actually experience that you are not your thoughts and emotions. Creating this distance will be helpful if you are trying to release negative energy or reduce stress and overtime you will find yourself "reacting" to life's challenges less and less. You will feel more centered, grounded, and present throughout your days and maintain an inner sense of peace, calm, and wellbeing.

Physical Movement

Physical Movement is a wonderful way to connect with the Life Force pulsating through all creation. Our true essence may be spirit, but we are living in a physical body. A wise Chinese proverb says, "Don't dig your well when you are dying of thirst." Maintaining and caring for your body will add much joy to your life and it's a great stress reliever as well. Try and find an activity that you enjoy and fits into your lifestyle. I have worked out my entire life and I have adjusted my exercise programs throughout. Cardio has always been the backbone of my workouts and my strength training has fluctuated to add some variety. When I was younger I was into body building and weight training. Then after I had back surgery in my forties I found Pilates to be very helpful in strengthening my core muscles, which also helped my back. Now in my fifties I practice Yoga and just started doing Qigong.

I remember trying to do Yoga and Qigong in my thirties,

but I was just too hyper. I wish I would have given it more time because they really focus on the body mind connection, which is now my favorite of all exercises. Yoga means union and it originated from India around 5000 years ago. The great thing about Yoga is there are so many levels, so regardless of your physical condition you can find a practice that will suit you. It focuses on awareness, flexibility, strength, mobility, relaxation, and balance. I just recently started doing Qigong which I feel will really benefit me as I age. Qigong originated from China around 4000 years ago and has been described as the "Art of effortless power." It's like a moving meditation helping you connect more deeply to the present moment. It helps circulate Chi which is the energy of life. When the life force energy circulates freely health and vitality are a natural side effect. Both these practices also involve breathwork which is a great way to connect with your spirit and release negative energy.

Appreciation

Living life in a state of appreciation is one of the most powerful things you can do to become a magnet for an abundance of good to flow into your life. Saying "Thank You" is the highest form of prayer and feeling appreciation for all the blessings in your life is going to attract more of the same. Sometimes if you are experiencing lower energies it may be difficult to feel gratitude, especially in regard to the situation or person you are struggling with. You probably want to clean up these negative emotions first, and then gradually work your way up to appreciation. The Emotional Release and Sooth and Uplift Letter that we reviewed in chapter five can help as well as affirmations and creative visualization. Meditation is also wonderful as when you are able to quiet your mind you are preventing the negative thoughts from building momentum. As you practice these techniques more and more you will start to intuitively know which one may be best for your circumstances.

Focusing on feeling appreciation will help you to maintain and build momentum with positive energy. There is always something you can find to give praise for such as: a warm gentle breeze, a loving smile, a beautiful sunset, your beating heart, the fragrance of a flower, a favorite song, and the list goes on. Starting with things we sometimes take for granted can get the energy flowing in the right direction and you can build from there.

Several years ago, I was leaving to go on a cruise when a terrible snowstorm started. The flight was scheduled to leave very early in the morning and the ship was leaving that same evening. Initially I wasn't concerned until I got to the airport and saw all the flights being cancelled. Despite it all I still did my best to maintain a positive attitude. I was visualizing myself arriving and texting everyone to let them know I made it. At the same time, I was imagining seeing my friend and I watching the Superbowl that was scheduled to air that evening while on the ship. We did board the plane which helped keep my spirits up, but then we ended up being on the runway for hours. There were electrical difficulties, and they were constantly de-icing the plane, and all the while the snow just kept coming down. Then the captain announced that there were about twelve planes ahead of us on the runway, that they were doing their best to take off, and only five percent of the flights would be getting out of O'Hare that day. Things were looking very bleak at that moment, however something in my energy instantly shifted after the captain made that announcement. I became swept over with feelings of gratitude and appreciation as I looked at all the employees working so hard so that these planes could take off. The plows, the air traffic controllers, the luggage handlers, the captain, and crew members all intent on getting us to our destination. I began sending thoughts of love and appreciation to all of them, feeling so grateful that all this effort was being made to get this flight out. I felt my vibration rising and rising and along with these feelings the plane started going faster and faster. It was one of the most blissful experiences in my life. It almost felt like my energy was lifting that plane right off the ground. So as you probably surmised, my flight did make it out and I did make my connection to the ship with very little time to spare. Only five percent of the flights made it out of O'Hare that that day, and mine was one of them. And, what's really awesome is when you have a demonstration like this manifest, you can always recall that experience at any time to give yourself an instant charge.

Expectations

Having expectations may not seem like action, but it

does take effort and discipline to maintain an expectant outlook, especially when your life may be reflecting something very different from what you are desiring. It's having the feelings of faith and trust in the absence of what you are wanting before any evidence comes to support it. The first step in developing an expectant attitude is letting go of the need to know how it will unfold. When you are able to do this you are opening up to an infinite number of possible ways your good can manifest, and the "how" is none of your business. It's like when you plant a seed, you don't dig it up after a week to see if it's growing, you trust that the process is taking place.

You will also want to "Act as If" your desire has already manifested. By doing this you will summon the emotions and energy of the desire. If it's a new car you want, go and take one for a test drive. If you want to go on a dream vacation, plan a day trip and embody the energy of being on vacation. If it's a new career, show up to your current job with the attitude you want to feel in your new chosen line of work, how you would relate to others, and how you would dress. This can really be a lot of fun and evoking the feeling of having achieved the desire is the first indicator that you are getting closer to a manifestation. When you are happy where you currently stand and joyfully expect your good to come forth, you are in a very powerful attraction point.

Another way of creating that feeling of expectancy is looking back over your past accomplishments and having faith in your ability to transform your energy. Savor your accomplishments and embrace all your successes. Know that you incarnated in this physical world to enjoy all its beauty, diversity, and pleasure. Relish in the unknown and ask the Universe to surprise you today. This is a fun way of releasing the need to know how something will unfold and create an energy of eagerness and enthusiasm about what is in store for you.

Have Fun

I was in my late teens when I first started attending a New Thought Church. I will never forget when I heard the minister, Dr Carleton Whitehead say, "Life is too important to be taken too seriously." Coming from a formal Catholic upbringing this was such a breath of fresh air, and from that moment on I claimed him as my first Guru. He was around 70 years old and along with his wisdom and knowledge he also possessed a fun playful spirit. At the time I was a pretty troubled teenager, but I took those words to heart and managed to maintain my sense of humor and lighthearted spirit throughout life's challenges.

Spending time on activities you enjoy really helps to nurture your spirit. Find out what makes your heart sing and make sure you plan time for it. Is it music, the arts, playing a sport, or traveling? We often get so busy with our daily lives that unless we intentionally set time aside for fun and recreation we can fill our schedule with work and other responsibilities. Leisure and relaxation are other activities that can really improve your quality of life.

It may sound self-indulgent, but these activities can assist in grounding you and create balance in your life. In this day and age it's so easy to be pulled in so many directions and this can have a huge impact on your energy alignment.

Another way to have fun is sharing your time with like-minded people. People who enjoy the same things you do and friends that motivate you and inspires you to be your best self. There is so much doom and gloom constantly being broadcasted everywhere you turn, surrounding yourself with individuals who are upbeat and positive will make it easier for you to maintain your positive energy. Taking a class can be a fun way to meet new people, and social media is filled with many resources to allow you to connect with others.

Laughter is healing and it's important to have fun with all this. When we are in the process of clearing negative energy we may be going through some growing pains, and that is perfectly natural. Just try your best to be easy about it and not get too engrossed. The more you can relax and have fun with this, the more you will begin to attract positive experiences. You and your life will always be changing and being happy and joyful in the moment is the main objective.

Action

Taking action can also be a way to align your energy and begin to build positive momentum. Let's say you have just started a diet and lost five pounds, that can be just the inspiration you need to stay on track. Even though you may have not reached your goal weight, being on the path and moving towards it brings you joy and keeps you motivated. Taking action from a place of happiness and inspiration is so much more productive than taking it from a place of lower energies. When you take action when you are feeling angry, revengeful, restless, depressed, or self-critical you are perpetuating that vibration in the action. Action taken from discontent emotions will only affirm the negative energy and practice it longer. For example you will often see people putting off their happiness until they attain a certain goal, meet that perfect person, or land that perfect job. They are never satisfied in the present and always waiting for some future event to happen. Or how often do you see someone who has numerous material possessions but has no time to enjoy them because they are too busy working to pay for them. In both these instances joy and contentment are not being experienced in the present and projected to some future date, and this becomes a vicious cycle.

Practicing "being present in the moment" is a fun skill to develop while taking action, and the practice of meditation can really assist you with this. As you quiet your thoughts, judgments, and labels you are allowing your spirit to shine through accompanying you in your experience. Colors will feel more vivid, food will taste better, and you will notice other people's spirits shining through as well. When you quiet the constant internal dialogue going on in your head you become more present for your life. You can start by practicing this for short periods of time and then increasing the duration. The more presence you bring into your everyday life the more you will begin to actually experience your life and not just be a bundle of conditioned responses and emotions.

Sometimes your path may not be a straight way forward, it can sometimes wind in a different direction or you may take a few steps backwards. Be flexible and open to the mystery of life, knowing you are in your perfect place. You are in the process of mastering skills and knowledge and who you become on this journey can never be taken away from you. The most important thing to keep in mind with action is the manifestation or final outcome is secondary compared to the way you feel in the attainment of it. And the more you live Everyday Magic you will find your actions start becoming a way of enjoying your manifestations. It feels like you are riding a wave and the Universe is totally supporting you while you are feeling exhilarated, alive, and present.

Chapter Highlights

- When you make it a priority to manage your personal energy first and foremost, your life will become more effortless, and you will start attracting people and circumstances that are in alignment with your desires and intentions.

- Making a decision is a great place to start in the action journey. Once you make a decision and line your energy and action up with it, the Law of Attraction has a clear signal to respond to.

- A very common conflict some people experience is that they lower their desire because they don't think what they want is possible.

- When you surrender you are not giving up your desires, but you are releasing the struggle and trying to control the outcome.

- It's a common misconception that when you forgive you are doing it to release the individual who you feel has harmed you, but really the person you are freeing is yourself.

- One of the greatest benefits from regular meditation is that you can give yourself some space from your thoughts and emotions, and you learn to gain more control over them.

- Physical Movement can be a great way to connect with the Life Force pulsating through all creation. Our true essence may be spirit, but we are living in a physical body.

- Saying "Thank You" is the highest form of prayer and feeling appreciation for all the blessings in your life is going to attract more of the same.

- The first step in developing an expectant attitude is letting go of the need to know how it will unfold. When you are able to do this you are opening up to an infinite number of possible ways your good can manifest, and the "how" is none of your business.

- Spending time on activities you enjoy really helps to nurture your spirit. Find out what makes your heart sing and make sure you plan time for it.

- The most important thing to keep in mind with action is the manifestation or final outcome is secondary compared to the way you feel in the attainment of it.

CHAPTER 8
Grace

Create a space for transformation to happen, for grace and love to enter. --Eckhart Tolle

Grace is not technically an ingredient in the Magic Potion, it is a biproduct of living Everyday Magic. It's like being a dancer and you rehearse and practice, but after a while the movements just flow beautifully, gracefully, and appear almost effortless. The same is true with the exercises and techniques in this book. They will assist you in gaining control of your emotions, thoughts, and beliefs so that you can allow the Divine Energy and Love to express more freely into your daily life. At first it may seem laborious, and it will require time and effort, but after a while your life starts to just flow with ease and grace. It can almost feel like there's a greater power and presence flowing through you, and your life becomes more about being than doing or having.

It's not that your life is free from challenges or difficulties, but you start to embrace them and appreciate how they are contributing to your growth and expansion. You come to understand the cycles of transformation, of birth, death, and rebirth, and celebrate the process. You also come to the realization that both the highs and lows are essential, and as wonderful as those peak moments are, it's not viable to sustain them permanently. If you did, they would no longer be a peak moment, and you would not be able to decipher them if it weren't for the contrasting experiences. Those special moments are times when we can praise ourselves and our Creator for having them and feel love and appreciation through all the colors of our life.

We also did not come to this physical world to deny it or be a bystander. We came here to experience the physical world and enjoy all the pleasures of it. We are here to enjoy the tastes, the senses, the touch, the feelings, the smells, and the beauty. There is nothing wrong with wanting to experience all the physical pleasure life has to offer. Physical manifestations are a great way to learn and develop our personal power and they also contribute to the expansion of the entire Universe. Enrichment also comes from having a sense of purpose and meaning, a feeling of belonging and a connection with others and a power greater than us.

As you move into this state of grace you start showing up as your authentic self, having the courage to live your truth. You feel empowered and creative, and your life becomes an extraordinary adventure. You treasure every moment and know your life is unfolding perfectly and gracefully. You not only feel supported by the Source of all creation, but you see that you are an avenue for it to express its greatness in the world. Maintaining connection to this Divine Energy is your primary intention, and the brighter you shine, the more light and love you bring to the world.

I recently watched a discussion with Deepak Chopra and Eckhart Tolle that really exhibited this whole idea of grace and divine synchronicity. Toward the end of the seminar they revealed that Wayne Dyer was in the audience, and they asked him to come up on stage. It just so happened that Dyer was also doing some type of workshop in that city, but he had no idea that Chopra or Tolle were there. When they accidentally crossed paths they invited Wayne to their seminar and what a moment it was to see these three men all on one stage together. It literally brought tears to my eyes, as I have such reverence and gratitude to each of them for assisting me along my spiritual path as well as raising the consciousness of humanity.

When we raise our consciousness it affects every person we encounter. As we learn to rise above the mundane chatter in our minds, our limiting beliefs, and our addictive emotional responses, we begin to allow our true spirit to express more freely through us. Everyday Magic is about personal transformation, and what that looks like is individual to each of us. It's a constant progression and expansion while at the same time feeling love and appreciation for the present moment and for who we are. Never underestimate how much influence you have by just being genuine and showing up embracing your weaknesses as well as your strengths.

I started learning these principles over 40 years ago and I'm still on my journey. I don't claim to be perfect or to have all the answers, I'm just sharing what I have found to be beneficial in my life. I hope the information and techniques offered in this book will assist you along your journey.

You are the world. When you transform yourself, the world you live in will also be transformed. --Deepak Chopra

ABOUT THE AUTHOR

When Gina turned 14 years old her mother gave her a book that would guide the rest of her life. The book was about the power of positive thinking and taking creative control of one's life. For more than forty years Gina has expanded her knowledge in all areas of personal development and transformation, applying this information in her life to achieve incredible results.

Gina developed a formula that she calls "The Magic Potion" which is just a fun way of describing the ingredients of the Creative Process. The formula expands on the concept of positive thinking, as it takes it to the next level of actually transforming your personal energy. Throughout this book Gina will guide you through the entire Creative Process while offering exercises and techniques that are easy to use and can be applied to any area of your personal development.

Everyday Magic has the power to transform you and your life. This book is your personal roadmap to living an enriched life filled with Joy and Abundance. Get ready to learn how to harness the Powers of the Universe to assist you in creating a life you have always dreamed of. Your journey begins here.

www.ingramcontent.com/pod-product-compliance
Lightning Source LLC
LaVergne TN
LVHW041221080426
835508LV00011B/1035